CHANGING WORLD, CHANGING CHURCH

THE REV. DR MICHAEL MOYNAGH was Policy Advisor on pay and then employment issues at the CBI before ordination into the Anglican Church. After serving as Team Rector of a lively parish in Somerset he is currently on the staff of St John's College, Nottingham. He is Co-Director of the Tomorrow Project and has written extensively on social issues.

'I am pleased to commend this book. It has made me ask, "Are people not Christian because they cannot believe, or because we have made it too hard for them to belong to our churches?" Every church leader should read it.'

– Canon Dr Christina Baxter, Chairman of House of Laity, Church of England General Synod

'The landscape is changing and the maps we once used to find our way are increasingly obsolete, but fortunately the compass still works. As the people of Jesus Christ we must survey the contours of this changing world, trust in him who never changes, and invent new forms of effective church for today. Mike's book serves us in this journey and so I commend it wholeheartedly to you.'

– Matt Bird, Director of Joshua Generation, author, speaker, consultant

'What Christianity in this country most needs is a renewal of imagination about the form of the church. It is time for a wide range of imaginative missionary initiatives that plant the gospel and the church where people are. I warmly endorse both Michael's cultural analysis and the missionary strategy proposed in this book. This is essential reading.'

– Rt Rev. Graham Cray, Bishop of Maidstone

'The Church Mission Society is appointing a senior staff member to promote a paradigm shift in how we do church in Britain. We urgently need new forms of church if we are to reverse the long-term decline in church-going in the UK, Western Europe and other parts of the Western World. This book is an essential guide to how church can be transformed.'

– The Rev. Canon Tim Dakin, General Secretary, Church Mission Society

'Without offering prescriptive models, Mike Moynagh succeeds in identifying new directions for the future – though there is a catch, for taking his argument seriously will require nothing less than the complete re-invention of the church as we know it. This is not a book for the faint-hearted, though visionaries and prophets will love it.'

– Rev. Dr John Drane, Head of Practical Theology, Aberdeen University

'This book is a must for anyone who thinks they know what church is all about. The idea that the church can be a one-stop-fits-all is quietly put to rest and a more dynamic image emerges.'

– Rev. Joel Edwards, General Director, Evangelical Alliance

'Whenever I hear Michael Moynagh speak, I get a tingling sense of excitement about the future. Michael's commitment to detailed scholarly research, his grasp of the issues which face the church today, and his love for the Lord, combine to make *Changing World, Changing Church* an essential companion for anyone who is seeking to shape the church of the New Millennium.'

– Rev. Dr Rob Frost, author and evangelist

'Anyone who is working in the church scene in the West will be aware of a feeling of dissatisfaction regarding the effectiveness of the church in today's world. How can the church change enough to make an impact in a society which seems to be uninterested in anything to do with "church"? Many ideas have come and some have gone and still the church is wallowing rather than swimming strongly. The "come and join us" approach no longer fits the it-must-fit-me world that we are living in. Michael Moynagh's book is not just another paperback on the same subject – read it, take heed, act on it and the church will never be the same again.'

– Rob Norman, Executive Director, Administry

'This is a book for all who are willing to consider a fresh approach to Christian mission and ministry. It is deceptively easy to read but if taken seriously could lead to radical changes in our understanding of how to be church. The ideas expressed do not, on the whole, demand great resources or big development pro-grammes but do need leaders and people willing to work in new ways. Above all the book is full of hope, based on confidence in the gospel, expressed in practi-cal theology and spiced with imagination and creativity. I warmly commend it.'

– The Reverend Baroness Richardson of Calow

'Do read it – now. It's urgent. By 2020 it will be too late.'

– Elaine Storkey, President of Tearfund, author and lecturer

'*Changing World, Changing Church* is a crucial book for rethinking the church in the 21st century. Where Mike Riddell left off Mike Moynagh takes us on.'

– Pete Ward, Lecturer in Youth Ministry and Theological Education, King's College, London

'If the church is to find a new lease of visible and public life in our society, we need both realism and a sense of urgency about its transformation. Not all essays on the renewal of the church combine these, but Michael Moynagh's crisply written book is a splendid example of how to put a challenge in a way that can be heard, bringing together some very clear analysis of our culture and a set of concrete and achievable steps that might be taken to meet the culture's needs without simply buying into its agenda. This is a really welcome book that should be read by every pastor and church leader – and every Christian committed to Christ's mission.'

– The Most Rev. Dr Rowan Williams, Archbishop of Wales

ADMINISTRY

Administry started out 20 years ago as an organisation helping churches be more effective in their mission by pointing out best practice in organisational methodology from a Christian viewpoint. Since then, there has been a very noticeable change in the church. However, there has been even more change in society and the church has often not kept up or even not noticed the widening gulf. In response to these factors, Administry has also changed.

We produce relevant publications, run practical training events and offer a unique consultancy advice on a whole range of areas of church life, but more importantly, yearn to see the changes in churches which Michael Moynagh is urging in this book. So much so that we have co-published this book with Monarch. We are also promoting a whole series of training events with Michael which will help churches engage with the issues of how churches need to change in order to be more effective.

To find out more about what we offer write to Administry, The Mega Centre, Bernard Road, Sheffield, S2 5BQ (UK), or phone 0114 278 0090 or e-mail mail@administry.co.uk

Changing World, Changing Church

- *New forms of church*
- *Out-of-the-pew thinking*
- *Initiatives that work*

MICHAEL MOYNAGH

MONARCH
BOOKS

Mill Hill London NW7 3SA and Grand Rapids, Michigan

First published by Monarch Books in 2001,
Concorde House, Grenville Place,
Mill Hill, London, NW7 3SA.

Published in conjunction with Administry

Distributed by:
UK: STL, PO Box 300, Kingstown Broadway, Carlisle,
Cumbria CA3 0QS;
USA: Kregel Publications, PO Box 2607,
Grand Rapids, Michigan 49501.

ISBN 1 85424 516 3 (UK)
ISBN 0 8254 6020 4 (USA)

British Library Cataloguing Data
A catalogue record for this book is available
from the British Library.

Designed and produced for the publishers by
Bookprint Creative Services
P.O. Box 827, BN21 3YJ, England
Printed in Great Britain.

CONTENTS

ACKNOWLEDGEMENTS

Most of the ideas in this book have been in the ether for a while, floating in one quarter or another either explicitly or implicitly. I am grateful therefore to countless people whose names I don't know.

I have benefited from conversations with Andy Aldridge, Martin Cavender, John Houghton, Drs Anne Richards and Stuart Murray, and the Rev'ds Tom Frame, Nicky Gumbel, Bob Hopkins, George Lings, Andrew Mawson, Steve Morgan and Kerry Thorpe, as well as from the consultations and interviews arranged under the auspices of the Tomorrow Project. Several people commented on a draft of the book, including Dr Christina Baxter, Dr Peter Brierley, the Preb. Francis Palmer, Dr Anne Richards and Richard Worsley.

I have spoken at a variety of seminars, conferences and other events, and on each occasion my thinking has been helped and provoked by the questions and comments I have received, not least from my students here at St John's which has proved a delightful place to work. I am grateful to all these, and to my wife, Liz, for her continuing encouragement. Shortcomings of the book are of course mine.

Michael Moynagh,
St John's Nottingham, January 2001

CHAPTER ONE

ONE CLICK FROM EXTINCTION

The *Harvard Business Review* is not most people's idea of a light read. But if you had flipped through the pages for July/August 1998, you would have come across an article by American management gurus Joseph Pine and James Gilmour, entitled 'Welcome to the experience economy'. In it they argued that the advanced world is racing into a new era.

Consumers have been getting bored. They go to the same old shopping malls, see the same old shops, view the same old brands, and they long for something new, something exciting, something that will arrest their interest. Retailers and manufacturers have developed a new line of business in response, experiences – and consumers love it.

Entertailing

British Airways, for example, is explicitly not in the business of selling journeys. It sells a distinctive experience of travel – one that enables the traveller to take time out from the frenetic pace of everyday life, recuperate, and arrive refreshed and ready to clinch that business deal.

More and more restaurants see their main activity as providing a particular experience of eating rather than selling food. At theme restaurants such as the Hard Rock Cafe, Planet Hollywood and the House of Blues, the food is just a prop for what is known as 'eatertainment'.

In one Los Angeles restaurant I visited, halfway through the meal the waiters and waitresses leapt on the bar and performed a tap dance routine, spinning the plates above their heads. New to this, I watched anxiously, wondering if my food would arrive on the plate or spin across the air! In Britain, Waddington's recently announced that it is to open a chain of 'Monopoly Cafes'.

Shopping itself is being transformed into an experience, with sights that titillate the eyes, subtle aromas and background music to create the right ambience. American stores such as Niketown, Cabella's and Recreational Equipment Incorporated draw in consumers by offering fun activities, fascinating displays and promotional events (sometimes dubbed 'shoppertainment').

Here comes the immersive world

Emerging technologies have encouraged whole new genres of experience, such as interactive games, Internet chat rooms and multi-player games, motion-based simulators and virtual reality. They are making it possible for people to become totally immersed in experiences. 'A Bug's Life' presentation at Disney World, for example, involves all the senses, including smells and creepy-crawly sensations under your legs.

As virtual reality becomes cheaper and more accessible, these experiences will be ever more sophisticated. We are entering not a visual culture (that was ushered in by television), but an immersive one.

The popular mantra is that over the past 200 years the 'Western' world has evolved from an agricultural economy to a manufacturing one, and now to an economy based on services. More true, however, is that the recent shift is from manufacturing to an experience economy.

Buying transformation

Nine months after their article, Pine and Gilmour published the book.[1] It contained the punch-line of their argument. Writing for a business audience, they asked what type of experiences would be most in demand. Their reply? Life-transforming experiences.

More and more people are seeking experiences that change them in some way – that make them feel better or look better, for example. So they will go to the gym and punish themselves for an hour, to emerge with a glow of achievement. Or they will acquire new skills from gliding to deep-sea diving, to become more interesting people. Or they will holiday abroad and study the culture of their destination to become more informed.

According to Pine and Gilmour, successful businesses will be those that market experiences which change people's lives.

And of course that is the business the church is in. For the past 2,000 years, far longer than the life of any corporation today, the church has offered people the opportunity to have their lives transformed – by Jesus Christ. As we hurtle into the new millennium, the very thing that our society craves – life transforming experiences – is at the centre of the church's mission statement. It's the heart of the gospel, a gospel astonishingly relevant to the experience economy. Could the new century be the church's century?

Going backwards

Yet as the Seattle-based futurist, Tom Sine reminds us, 'We are going backwards not forwards in global evangelisation. 28% of the world's people would identify themselves as Protestant, Catholic or Orthodox today. By the year 2010 that will decrease to 27% and continue to decline from there because the global

Yet again, lack of a congregation was hampering the verger's fund-raising drive.

population is growing more rapidly than the global church.'[2] The trends are especially gloomy in the West – and, despite what some think, that includes the United States.

The vanishing church show in Britain

Church attendance has plummeted in Britain. In 1979 5.4 million people in England attended church on an average Sunday. Ten years later that number had dropped to 4.7 million. Nine years later, in 1998, the total had collapsed to 3.7 million. A 13% decline over ten years was followed by a staggering 22% fall over nine years.[3]

Some people take comfort from attendance at church midweek. Figures for Sunday, they say, exaggerate the speed of decline. More people are going to church on weekdays. But there have always been midweek services. The number switching to weekday church is a tiny drop in the ocean of all church-goers. It barely dents the vast haemorrhage from Sundays. 'Good news! There are slightly more on the Titanic than we thought'[4] is hardly encouraging.

Others claim the figures are not as bad as they seem because people are still committed to church, they just go less often. Sunday attendance is down because more people are going once or twice a month instead of every week. This is part of a bigger picture. Up to the 1960s it was not uncommon for many people to attend church twice on a Sunday. Since then 'two-timers' have almost completely disappeared. Now we are told that once a Sunday is giving way to once every few weeks.

This can scarcely be good news for the church. It suggests that the faithful are becoming less committed. With so many other pressures on people's time, church is being squeezed out. Will we find that people attend church less and less often, till they stop going altogether?

More hope for Australia?

If the news is bad in Britain, it is not much better in Australia. In 1950 44% of the population attended church once-monthly or more. Today the figure is just 10%, 1.8 million people. There are signs that the nosedive bottomed out in the 1990s, but not that it has gone into reverse.

Indeed, the picture may be rather flattering. Church numbers have been lifted by successive waves of immigration. Many newcomers arrived with Christian backgrounds and have continued to attend ethnically-based churches. As they become more integrated into mainstream society, their children are likely to pick up the non-churchgoing habits of their Australian friends.

Not much comfort for the United States

This seems to be the story behind the continued health of church attendance figures in the United States. Black, Hispanic and Asian congregations are growing at a significant rate. But with the exception of the Catholic Church, virtually all the mainline denominations are in decline. In 1968 eleven mainline Protestant denominations represented 13% of the US population. By 1993 this had spiralled down to 7.8% – a 40% drop. If the present trends continue uninterrupted these churches will be totally out of business by 2032.

Some of this decline is being offset by new churches like The Vineyard, but even growing denominations saw their growth rates slow between 1985 and 1993. The portion of the American population involved in church actually declined over that eight-year period.

Over the past ten years Barna Research reports that while older generation attendance ranged from roughly 40% to 60%, the Buster generation (born between 1965 and 1983) came in at 34%. Even these figures may be optimistic. Kirk Hadaway, chief statistician for the United Church of Christ, has convincing evidence that Americans are over-reporting their attendance.[5]

The 'incredibly shrinking church' in Britain and Australia is set to become a reality in the United States as well. Pockets of growth cannot hide the gradual erosion of church across swathes of the population.

Time for a rethink

There is no time for complacency. Peter Brierley of Christian Research notes that church attendance figures in England are alarming not just because they are declining, but because the rate of decline is speeding up. If the rate of change continues, the percentage of people in England going to church in 2016 would be down to 0.9%! 'Just one generation, and we would indeed have bled to death.'[6]

Of course, you cannot project today's trends into the future unchanged. Lots can happen to make a difference. Trends can get worse! They can also get better, but they won't get better automatically. Something has to happen to produce the change. What would have to occur to restore the vanishing church not only in Britain, but in other advanced societies?

Church has lost its way

Certainly in Britain, New Zealand and elsewhere there is growing recognition that we cannot go on as we are. Many clergy and lay people know that today's church is not working, it is not connecting with people any more, but they cannot imagine anything different. They struggle on with tried and trusted methods, feeling uneasy but with little vision for how things could change.

Others are busting a gut to make existing churches grow, sometimes succeeding, but often wearing themselves out – and their congregations! – instead. They hear about 'successful' churches and think, 'If it can work for them, surely the same approach will work for us'. They ignore how different their circumstances are, or how beacon churches often achieve growth by drawing Christians away from smaller churches. What will happen to these 'successful' churches when their small-church feeder-systems dry up?[7]

Still other ministers look back to the 1970s and '80s, desperately hoping to repeat what was effective then. But the world has moved on, and so frequently they are disappointed. They burn out, exhausted and disillusioned because they see so little fruit.

A few leaders are trying fresh forms of church – imaginative experiments which may in time blaze a route to a radically different church that reconnects with the world. These pioneers are responding intuitively to opportunities around them, but sometimes they feel alone and wonder how far their efforts fit into the larger whole.

Finding a new path

This is a book about why the church need not disappear, and how we can lay the foundations of substantial growth. It is a book therefore for those who are committed to church.

Yet for many people church is the last thing they want. They might feel offended to think that we are trying draw them in. If our approach was in any way patronising ('we've got the answers, you haven't'), or at all manipulative ('we'll make friends with you but only to get you to church'), or lacking respect ('we're more keen to talk about our faith than to listen to yours'), then our attitude would indeed be offensive.

Our task is not to press people into church. Rather, church is a gift. We can make it more attractive. We can offer it to people. But we must respect each person's decision as to whether it is a gift for them.

This is a book, then, not about intrusive evangelism, but about how church can be made attractive to those who might want it.

The shape of the book

The book is in two halves. First, we shall look at some epoch-making trends that will shape our society over the next 20 years, and which church leaders – ordained and lay – need to understand if they are to take society by storm.

The template of daily life is changing as we move from standardised society to an it-must-fit-me world. Even more than today, life will be about managing choice. It will be about jumping between consumer and workplace modes of thought, which are very different to each other. How will the church make contact with this emerging world and the tensions within it? Today's church has become disconnected from people, but it will have huge opportunities to make contact in future.

The second part of the book describes how the church can grow once again. It starts with a vision of the church in 2020 –

a church that has become highly responsive to the different fragments of society, and eager to network those fragments together. It describes how this future is today becoming a reality in some of the new forms of church that are being trialled. These experiments could herald a dramatic shift in evangelistic strategy – one that builds new expressions of church for a new era.

This strategy can draw on lessons from society, but it needs to be driven by Scripture. So chapter 10 runs the strategy through a biblical X-ray to confirm that its roots are indeed in Scripture. We then ask how new believers – as part of this strategy – can be helped to become agents of social change.

The book concludes with some practical steps that smaller churches, larger ones and denominational leaders can all take. These steps would replace a 'you come to us' church with one that comes to you. In an it-must-fit-me world, they would create a church that fits – both people and God.

So mission equals evangelism?

Does this mean that evangelism must be an absolute priority for church? Some would say so. Others would claim that the church's mission is much bigger than that – that the church's central task is to bring society closer to God's values. Questions of justice may take priority over evangelism.

Others again would feel more comfortable with the idea that God is active outside the church – that just as he used rulers in the ancient world to achieve his purposes (e.g. Isaiah 45:1) so he continues to work in the world to advance his cause. The church's central task is not to colonise society for God, but to attend to what God is already doing in the world.

All these perspectives have important insights, and the church will be most healthy when they are woven together. The focus on evangelism in this book is just one aspect of the church's much broader mission.

Learning from the future

To sharpen our focus we shall draw heavily on the work of the Tomorrow Project, which has been researching the future of people's lives in Britain over the next two decades. Backed by companies, charitable trusts and government departments, the Project has examined ten aspects of people's lives, including 'People, faith and values'.

Some 200 experts have been interviewed, including experts outside Britain, and ten two-day consultations have been held involving eminent researchers, policy-makers, practitioners and people from the media – around 20 at each consultation. The initial results were published in May 2000 as *Tomorrow*,[8] which was distributed to 50,000 key decision-makers and opinion-formers in the public, private and voluntary sectors.

The research has yielded a megabase of societal trends which reflect developments not only in Britain, but in the global economy. Even the UK data has planet-wide significance because much of what is happening in Britain echoes the advanced world as a whole.

If we are to evangelise advanced society, we need a fresh mission strategy – a different framework that can channel our prayers and our initiatives to more fruitful ends. Nothing less than a makeover will equip the church to reach the changing world that is emerging so rapidly before our eyes.

Notes

1 B. Joseph Pine and James H. Gilmour, *The Experience Economy*, Harvard Business School Press, 1999.

2 Tom Sine, *Mustard Seed versus McWorld*, Monarch, 1999, p. 177.

3 Peter Brierley, *The Tide is Running Out*, Christian Research, 2000, p. 27.

4 Comment by the Revd Bob Jackson, lecture, 19 October 2000.

5 Sine, *op. cit.*, pp. 186–191.
6 Brierley, *op. cit.*, p. 28.
7 Eddie Gibbs, *ChurchNext*, IVP, 2000, p. 42.
8 Copies can be obtained from LexiCon Editorial Group Services, 1–5 Clerkenwell Road, London, EC1M 5PA, UK. Phone 020 7253 5775. Fax 020 7253 5676. E-mail activelife@lexicon-uk.com.

CHAPTER TWO

HELLO, IT-MUST-FIT-ME WORLD

Go into Starbucks, the American coffee house chain now expanding round the world, ask for a cup of coffee and they will think you are mad. 'Excuse me, sir, is that cafe latte, cappuccino or expresso? Do you want the New Guinea Peaberry or the Guatamala something else?' The choice is vast – so great it leaves some people paralysed. Fortunately, they can choose 'coffee of the day'.

Starbucks is so large that it can use its huge size to bulk-buy, at bargain-basement prices, coffees to suit all tastes. It is an example of how the second stage of the consumer revolution is transforming our lives, almost unnoticed.

The new consumerism

The first stage, mass consumption, swept through the United States between the wars and into Europe in the 1950s. Firms used the advantages of size to expand the range of standardised products that people could buy. A large supermarket today may stock 22,000 product lines or more. Once you have selected the product, one item is much the same as another. Apart from differences in size, each packet of Kellogg's cornflakes is the same.

A glove, not a straitjacket

The second stage of the consumer revolution, mass customisation, began to have an impact in the 1980s. More and more companies are using size to tailor products more closely to the demands of individuals or small groups of customers. One of Britain's insurance companies, Legal and General, promised, 'You can choose the level of cover that suits you.'

Mass customisation is advancing so rapidly that it is about to become the defining feature of our consumer world. Look at a Ford assembly line and you will find that almost every car has the name tag of its future owner. The trims and fittings have been customised to match the preferences of scores of different buyers.

In some of the Levi stores you can go into a booth, have your body measurements taken by laser, the numbers are sent down the wire to a factory miles away, and two or three weeks later a pair of jeans, made to fit your exact body measurements, is delivered to your front door.

Dell Computers web-site links customers directly with the production line. Place an order on the site, it will go straight to production, and you can sit back and wait for the PC to be delivered to your door. No need for people in sales, inventory or retailing. Customers can enter their own specifications and know that their customised PCs will be delivered at rock-bottom prices. The customer becomes a partner in designing the exact computer required. This will become standard for many products. Musicmaker.com, for example, allows you to order a CD with your own selection of tracks on it.

In some ways it feels the way it did before the industrial revolution, when goods were crafted to the client's exact requirements. The big difference is that this attention to the individual is now being combined with low-cost production secured by the benefits of scale. A vast range of personalised goods can be brought to a wide market.

Four Faces of Customisation – how American firms go about customisation

Collaborative customisers dialogue with each customer to help them choose exactly what they want. So for example at Custom Foot in Westport, Connecticut, a salesperson will take your measurements using a digital foot imager, you will be shown a variety of design elements such as different toes and different heels, you make your choice and the final specifications are dispatched electronically to Italy, where the shoes are custom-made.

Adaptive customisers offer a standard product that is designed for users to alter themselves. Select Comfort of Minneapolis, Minnesota, for instance, designs and manufactures mattresses with air chamber systems that do more than automatically contour to the bodies of those who lie on them: users can adjust the levels of firmness, changing them from night to night if they want and selecting different levels for both sides of the bed.

Cosmetic customisers present a standard product differently to different customers. The product may be packaged specially for each customer, for example, as with the Hertz #1 Club Gold Program. You still get the same basic car, but you bypass the line at the counter. The shuttle bus takes you to a canopied area where you see your own name in lights on a large screen which directs you to the exact location of your car. The car's boot is open, your name is displayed on the personal agreement hanging from the mirror and where weather and law permits the engine is running, waiting for you.

Transparent customisers give individuals unique goods and services without letting them know explicitly that these products have been customised for them. The Ritz-Carlton for instance observes the preferences guests show during each stay. Do they switch to a classical radio station, select chocolate chip cookies and prefer hypoallergenic pillows? The information is used to tailor the service the customer receives next time they visit. The more often you stay at its hotels, the more the company learns and the more

> customised goods and services are fitted into its standard rooms.
> It is hoped that this will make the hotel the guests' preferred
> choice.[1]

Consuming everything

Consumerism sets the tone for so much of our lives that, not surprisingly, this new stage of the consumer revolution will affect almost every aspect of our existence.

In education, for example, California's Stanford Research Institute is developing distance-learning packages in which modules will be broken into ten-minute segments. You will be able to do two segments on a train journey, and perhaps one in a taxi ride – learning when and where you want. Keeping this material up to date will be expensive, and so education providers are likely to combine together to reduce overheads. Just-in-time education – learning when you want – will be made possible by the advantages of size.

In health, the human genome project is organised internationally. Pharmaceutical companies are rushing to transform its results into a revolutionary new generation of drugs, which will be targeted at the particular genetic make-up of individuals and small groups of patients. In the process the companies are merging to pool research and development. Once again, scale is being used to provide a more individualised approach.

In church the phenomenally successful Alpha course, which boasted over one-and-a-half million participants in the 1990s, offers a ten–week introduction to Christianity. Material is produced centrally and supported by national advertising campaigns. Yet courses are organised by local churches to fit their particular circumstances. The highlight of each one is a day or weekend away, when participants are encouraged to have their own, individual experiences of God. Many report that this was a turning point in their lives.

Organisations are relating to people in a more personalised way, and the same trend is starting at work.

The new workplace

One certainty about the future is that people won't spend all week behind computer screens working from home. They may stay home for one or two days a week, but not for the whole time.

That is because the benefits of being together at work are too great – the feeling of being involved, the chance to make friends, the chit-chat by the vending machine which can spark a bright idea, the building of trust by seeing people in different contexts, the protection of confidential information (which organisation allows its treasured secrets into people's homes?) and managing stress, which is aggravated by isolation and lack of social support. There are huge advantages in being present in a larger work group.

Made-to-measure work

What is changing is how these benefits are becoming tailored to the individual. Sometimes this is happening in small ways. More employers are encouraging staff to dress down, giving individuals more choice over what they wear. Even in factory-like call centres, attempts to personalise work are being tried. In some centres employees have been grouped into small units to give a stronger 'family' feel, while in one or two cases staff have been given much greater control over what they do.

More significant perhaps is the greater discretion being offered to some employees over when, where and how they work. Some organisations are allowing staff more choice over when to work at home and in the office, and whether to work through the day or – from time to time – in the afternoon and evening.

In London a 'Timecare' computer programme has been set up for nurses. It allocates shifts according to when nurses are most in demand and when they want to work. Nurses' requests for time off are logged on a computer, which keeps a record of the hours they have worked. If someone would prefer to work for five hours but has to work for eight, the three extra hours are banked with the computer and added to time off later. The more surplus hours a nurse banks, the more favourably will the computer treat requests for time off. Nurses have more flexibility in choosing which shifts to work.[2]

Employed to be self-employed

Payment-by-results is spreading, with performance-linked bonuses a larger component of many people's income. More jobs are being franchised – such as counter operations within retailers. These developments herald a significant trend. Most people will still work for a single organisation, but their work will feel more like self-employment. People will be paid for the tasks they perform rather than the hours they actually work.

Teachers for example may contract to achieve certain test and exam results. Targets would be set according to what could be reasonably expected of pupils in the particular school. Teachers would agree to teach so many pupils and secure a standard set of results. Those who beat the target would get a bonus, while those who under-performed would be paid less. Teachers would be paid for a task, just as a self-employed plumber might be hired for a particular job, rather than for the time they put in. The spread of performance-related pay in many schools may be a first step towards this.

Personal assistants may be hired to perform specified assignments. How they organise those tasks, when they are in the office and when they work from home, and the hours they actually work would be up to them, so long as the tasks were performed to their boss's satisfaction. They would be responsible for managing their own work, as if they were self-employed.

We are moving from mass production where workers were treated in a standardised way to the 'individualised organisation',[3] where employees are given more opportunity to be themselves and to manage their own work. The benefits of working in a larger group are combined with greater personal freedom.

The recent change in teachers' pay creates some unexpected problems.

Leaner, meaner and faster than ever

A similar pattern lies behind the spread of 'networked organisations'. In recent years organisations have been breaking down into smaller components, with each unit having greater independence.

This will continue. Sometimes this will be through more outsourcing – buying in services instead of supplying them inhouse – which allows organisations to focus on what they do best. Sometimes it will be through decentralisation to give individual units greater discretion. The different elements of an organisation end up with more freedom to specialise, to develop their own strategies and to respond quickly to the market.

At the same time networking will continue to make available the benefits of size. Separate firms may work together to share research and development costs. An entire supply chain may operate as a single unit, exchanging information and working collaboratively to secure just-in-time delivery, raise quality and gain other efficiencies. Potential competitors may cooperate in dividing up the market, to guarantee each company a larger share.

Companies will collaborate so that buying an airline ticket on the Internet, for example, will become a gateway to other services. When you get your ticket, you will not only buy insurance as now, but other services such as a hotel reservation, advice on quality restaurants and a theatre ticket in the city of destination. This is already beginning to happen, and we shall see plenty more examples. Cooperation makes what each organisation has to offer more attractive.

The emerging 'network society' combines the advantages of scale through collaboration with more freedom for organisations to play to their strengths. It is a trend that is affecting every sphere – the public, private and voluntary sectors, not to mention the media. There is no future in going it alone: you can do more to achieve your goals if you work with others.

Churches who often struggle to work together have much to learn. As we shall see, cooperation will be vital if church is to connect with the emerging world.

www.newgovernment.gov

Mass consumption and mass production were accompanied by mass government. The government treated people in a standardised way – the rules for one person were the same for everyone. No wonder bureaucracy became a dirty word: people wanted to be treated as individuals. But this is beginning to change, and the pace is hotting up.

Customised government

Governments in the advanced world are rapidly transferring their services on-line. Tax returns are just one example. They can now be dispatched on-line and enquiries sent electronically to the tax office. The door is opening to a more individualised relationship with government. People won't have to wait till office hours, they will be able to communicate electronically with government whenever they want.

It is widely recognised that social exclusion is best tackled by gearing the resources of the community to the varying needs of individuals. In parts of Australia for instance a social worker, paid for by the community, will actually live for a time with a dysfunctional family, helping members to change their patterns of behaviour, before gradually withdrawing – the ultimate in personalising community support.

Down to the local

Likewise, all the main political parties play lip-service to the importance of taking local differences into account when framing policy. Education, employment and health action zones in Britain give expression to this. They are designed to foster local solutions to local problems.

But how can a local focus be combined with the coordination of resources at state or national levels? A national (or state) tax system with uniform rates harnesses the wealth of the better-off to support those in need. It is highly efficient. Imagine the extra costs of myriad local taxes, each with their own bureaucracies! But it also gives great power to central government. Using that power to increase local discretion remains an immense challenge.

This will top the political agenda in the years ahead as government continues to decentralise, especially in Britain. In the UK, devolution of powers to Northern Ireland, Scotland and Wales, a newly elected mayor for London and the possible election of mayors in other cities has begun to reverse the centralisation of government. This process is almost certain to continue, forcing government to become more sensitive to the different priorities of different areas.[4]

The challenge will be to combine the advantages of greater local control with the benefits of doing some things centrally. What is best done centrally and what locally? How local is local – city level or regional? Where is the centre – in the case of Britain, Westminster or Brussels? And how should the different levels of government interact?

In short, how can the benefits of scale be combined with the advantages of customisation?

Customising the Cabinet?

Perhaps the ultimate in customised government would be a customised Cabinet. Instead of having Cabinet ministers for Education, Health, Social Security and the like, ministers would speak for particular client groups – the elderly, children, the unemployed and so on.

Ministers would order services from existing government departments and bundle them together so that they were suitable for their clients. The Minister for Disabled People for example would order health, education and other services, and ensure that they were designed appropriately.

A far-fetched idea? The UK is taking small steps toward this, with the appointment of Cabinet ministers to champion women and older people, in addition to their existing briefs. Might we see, in time, further steps towards this?

A sea-change

So we are witnessing a major shift in the tectonic plates of society. Everywhere we turn, the same trend is at work. We are moving from an off-the-peg to a tailor-made world.

In the off-the-peg society, scale was used to produce

standardised products, to treat workers in a standardised way, to develop standardised organisations and to deliver standardised government that was roughly the same in every place. In the tailor-made world scale will be used to customise products, to treat workers in a more individualised way, to develop networks in which independent organisations share resources and to deliver government services that will increasingly vary from place to place.

A long journey remains. Many attempts to personalise organisations are clumsy and unconvincing. Call centres for example, in the name of good service, leave consumers pressing one phone button after another. When they eventually speak to an operator, customers scream because their particular question can't be answered. Genuinely personalised service seems miles away. But as more organisations leave standardisation behind, they will become better skilled in relating to individuals in a personalised way.

How will organisations use these relationships – to serve people or exploit them?

Size with *individualism*

Two features of our society, then, are coming together. One is the importance of size, reflected for example in company mergers, in organisations which are networking so that they can pool their resources, in global marketing, in the emergence of regional groupings like the European Union, and in the widespread feeling that the world is becoming so big and complex that we can scarcely understand it. 'A big world needs a big bank' claimed a recent UK commercial.

The other is the growing individualisation of society. Values are a matter of personal preference. The individual must be allowed to choose. It's up to you . . .

In mass society, size and the individual were often pitted against each other. Workers felt like cogs in a machine. The individual was treated in a uniform way. Today we are crossing a watershed as scale is increasingly used to expand individual choice and to help individuals secure exactly what they want. Size and the individual are working more closely together – at least on the surface. We have entered the age of personalised scale – an it-must-fit-me world.

Tailor-made for post-modernity

A post-modern mindset will be at home in this new world. Though the term 'post-modern' is complex and has sparked much debate, one of its key features is the view that we must not universalise truth, we must not describe the world with one big story, because in doing so we may fail to hear – and even stifle – dissenting views. The 'big story' of male hierarchy, it is said, marginalised the very different stories of women.

This central tenet of the post-modern mindset has a struc-ture which matches that of personalised scale. Whatever post-modernists say, within the post-modern outlook there *is* a big story. Paradoxically, what that big story says is that there are no big stories. It is a big story which legitimises 'little stories'. It compels us to pay attention to different stories and not to smother them with claims of universal truth. It validates the approach, 'You decide'.

In other words, scale – the post-modern big story – is being used to give individuals greater freedom, freedom to have their own views of the world and for these views to be heard. It is a scale serving the person.

Four spotlights on 'New Times'

Many people think that we are entering 'new times', as radically different to the past as the industrial revolution was to the agricultural world that preceded it. What will these 'new times' look like? Four ways of describing them emphasise four different features.

Knowledge is emphasised by those who think that the information revolution will be central to the new world. Essential to this revolution is knowledge. We shall spend more and more on buying knowledge – from recipe books to TV travel programmes, or on buying products whose value is based on knowledge, such as the service of a fitness instructor. 'The real assets of the modern economy come out of our heads not out of the ground: ideas, knowledge, skills, talent and creativity.'[5]

Networks are stressed by those who believe that the communications revolution will be central to the new world. People across the globe are becoming connected in new ways, and this will transform our lives – even more so when we can communicate visually both on-line and by mobile phone. What people crave through the new media is not so much knowledge as fresh opportunities to be in touch with others. New networks will give rise to a new society. See Manuel Castells, *The Rise of the Network Society,* Blackwell, 1996.

Fragmentation perhaps lies at the heart of post-modern perspectives. Shared values that hold society together are giving way to a pluralistic world, in which a variety of beliefs rub shoulders with each other. As global forces lift power further and further away from the individual, people will increasingly identify with their physical neighbourhood, or with an ethnic group or with groups that share a common interest. These will provide meaning, belonging and security in a complex, alien and risky world. Central to this is the rise of the consumer culture with its emphasis on choice. Krishan Kumar, *From Post-Industrial to Post-Modern Society*, Blackwell, 1995 provides a useful introduction.

Personalised-scale has been a focus of the Tomorrow Project. It owes much to 'Post-Fordist' thinkers who argue that society has moved beyond the mass-produced, standardised models that Ford automobiles used to epitomise. Mass production and mass organisation have reached their limits. Mass society, with mass working class movements such as trade unionism, is breaking down. Instead we are seeing flexible, customised production and new social movements, often of a local kind. *Tomorrow* (LexiCon, 2000) argues that central to 'new times' is a more personalised relationship between organisations and people.

Each of these spotlights need to be shone together to see the full picture.

What will drive these changes?

When they talk about forces of change in the advanced world, most experts refer to globalisation, post-modern values, demographics and technology. Each of these will accelerate the arrival of the it-must-fit-me world.

Globalisation involves the interlocking of nations so that they begin to form a single unit. It will persistently widen markets and create economies of scale. Big will get even bigger, allowing endless new brands to find their niche. This will widen people's choice. Only two or three people in a city may like a particular song, but if it is two or three people in every city throughout the world then that becomes a sizeable audience! Individuals will be offered a stunning expansion of routes to personal fulfilment.

Post-modern values include the rejection of hierarchy, suspicion of institutions and strong emphasis on personal choice. They have largely grown out of the inconsistency of mass society. The mass world expanded the range of choice – you could choose between ever more options – but continued to treat people in a standardised way. People were left dissatisfied.

Inevitably, once they had some choice they wanted more. Having tasted choice they became irritated by one-size-fits-all and suspicious of top-down organisations which squeezed them into a mould. Mass society contained the seeds of its own demise. The post-modern mindset took hold – and is now itself a force for change. It is highly receptive to personalised scale.

Demographics will be important, first because older people will be more numerous – and also more affluent. They will have had a lifetime of rising consumer expectations. So they will be delighted to spend their time and money on more personalised products, which will jack up their expectations further. They certainly won't want uniform treatment.

Secondly, younger people will be better educated, with many more staying longer at school and going to university. Higher education tends to take working class people beyond their background, by equipping them for better paid jobs and exposing them to a wider range of values. More young people will have the money to pay for a personalised lifestyle and will be set free from the traditions of home, free to choose between the values of the emerging world. Sadly, the poor will be left behind.

Technology will continue to make personalised scale possible, symbolised by the Internet itself – the more people who use it, the more each person can find precisely what they want.

New age, new mindset

As we gallop towards the it-must-fit-me world, people's mindsets will change. If your drugs fit you exactly, if your mortgage fits your exact circumstances, if you can find precisely what you want on the Net, you will end up expecting everything to fit you exactly.

'Well, it's not the same with the new minister. Church isn't what it used to be. (It doesn't fit me exactly any more.) Time to move on.' 'My marriage doesn't feel quite the same (she no longer fits me exactly). Perhaps we should separate.' The attitude has already crept up on us. It will become yet more pronounced.

If you want to know how people will be thinking as we dash into the new century, 'it must fit me exactly' is the answer. It will be the defining outlook of personalised scale.

From 'it-must-fit-me' to 'I must fit you'

It is an attitude that will sideline the Bible's central concern with justice. If people's reference point is what fits them perfectly, there will not be much room in their hearts for those who feel socially edged-out and who cannot afford it-must-fit products. We risk becoming a more selfish society. This makes the task of evangelism and discipleship even more urgent. How can we revolutionise our culture with the gospel of grace – a gospel that transforms 'fit me' into a willingness to fit others?

But it is also an attitude that echoes parts of the gospel. God who is infinitely great wants to connect with us in a personalised way. He wants his love to be made-to-measure – to draw out the best in us and help us achieve our potential. He doesn't want my relationship with him to be precisely the same as yours. That is why Christians have such different experiences of God. God's love fits each person exactly.

So as we speed into the new century, the challenge for the church will be to help people see how their it-must-fit-me-exactly mindset resonates with parts of the gospel, to walk with them on their journey into Christ's love and to stand by them as this love, painfully sometimes, transforms their expectation from 'It must fit me' to 'I must fit you'.

A church that fits?

To do this the church itself will need to change. By and large, the church is still stuck in the standardised world. It approaches evangelism with a mass mindset. 'Come and join our church' is the invitation, which assumes that 'our church' is suitable for the people we invite. 'We like it so other people will.' That is typical one-size-fits-all thinking.

The church could get away with it in mass society, but in an it-must-fit-me world it won't wash any more. A different approach is needed – one that is more sensitive to the differences between people, to their suspicion of organisations and to their expectation of choice. The reaction of other organisations is to draw closer to people, to listen to them and to respond to their individual preferences. Can the church afford to stand aloof?

In 1995 an Anglican and a Baptist church in Bristol, England jointly launched a three monthly 'seeker service' for older people who did not come to church. The services included drama, an interview, two well-known hymns, a secular song on the theme, and tea – loads of it. They discovered three specific needs – a place to belong, a sense of family and a place which is linked with hope for the future.

Those who came wanted the seeker services more often. That was not practical, but a small team started a fortnightly Focus Group with a simpler programme – generally a speaker, sharing family news, a hymn and some prayer, followed by food. Here was a realistic response to the needs of a specific group of people. Instead of hoping that older people on the fringe would come to established church, church was built round them and their particular needs. Church was 'customised'.

Was this a sell out to consumer values? Or was it the church becoming more people-shaped without losing its God-shape?

Notes

1 James H. Gilmore and B. Joseph Pine II, 'The Four Faces of Mass Customization', *Harvard Business Review*, January–February 1997, pp. 91–101.

2 Reported in *The Times*, 23 February 1998.

3 Sumantra Ghoshall and Christopher A. Bartlett, *The Individualised Corporation*, Heinemann, 1999.

4 Robert Hazell (ed.), *Constitutional Futures. A History of the Next Ten Years*, OUP, 1999.

5 Charles Leadbeater, *Living on Thin Air*, Penguin, 1999, p. 18.

CHAPTER THREE

CHOICE BUSTERS

At the end of a talk about tailor-made consumerism, one person exclaimed, 'Don't you agree that what Mike has given us is not a vision of the future, but a vision of sheer hell! All this choice! How on earth will we cope?'

Option paralysis

It was a good question. As organisations relate to people in a more personalised way, we shall face a torrent of choice. Which school shall I send my child to? Should my holiday have an educational focus or shall I just chill out? Would I prefer to have physiotherapy or try an osteopath? Where shall we eat tonight? Critics will complain that many of these choices will be trivial or manipulated, but even so we shall still be bombarded by choice.

Choice has become central to the new style of 'democratic' parenting. It is no longer 'Time for tea kids, it's hamburgers' but, 'What would you like for tea tonight, hamburgers or hot-dogs?' Children are showered with alternatives. They are growing up with choice central in their lives.

Of course choice fatigue has not hit everyone. Many people are denied choice because of poverty and other forms of deprivation, and sadly that will persist. But for an increasing number of people user-chooser will be the norm. The shift to personalised scale will confront them with a staggering array of possibilities. Each day they will be bewildered by an ever-expanding menu of it-must-fit-you-exactly alternatives. Steering a path through the options will become a central pre-occupation. Even more than today, life will be about managing choice.

This will affect organisations that are seeking a more person-alised relationship with their users. If they are creating more choices so that individuals can have exactly what they want, they will need to help people manage that choice. Organisations will have to draw close to people they serve, listen to them and help them make up their mind. How will they do this, and will there be lessons for the church?

Agents, agents everywhere!

The use of agents – intermediaries who narrow down the options and help you choose – will be one strategy. They are already an essential part of our lives. Travel agents, for example, help you select from a host of offers by displaying holidays in glossy catalogues and providing advice. Realtors or estate agents help you choose a property. Financial advisers, sales staff and many others play a similar role.

Types of agent

Expect these agents to mushroom in the years ahead. They will take many forms. There will be human agents such as the new breed of shopping advisers, and there will be electronic agents, of which today's search engines on the Net are a foretaste. There will also be hybrid agents – human agents who use computers to help their clients. 'Please wait a moment, I'll check on-line that we have covered all the possibilities, and then we can discuss what's going to be best for you'.

Shopping in 2020

The year is 2020 and it is my mother's eightieth birthday. I instruct my agent to assemble a display of gifts for an older woman. Putting on my virtual reality glasses, the size of today's spectacles, I 'go into' my digital TV and rove round a virtual store brimming with goods for older people. I spot a collection of headscarves, admire one and, speaking into the TV (the technology will allow that), ask for the price and where it can be found. I then pop down to the shopping centre, check how the scarf feels and that its colour in real life matches its colour in virtual reality, and make my purchase. Thanks to my electronic agent, I've saved myself a whole afternoon traipsing around the shops!

No one is sure exactly how people will shop in the future, but something on those lines is very much within the realms of possibility. The electronic agent will play a key role.

Agents will become a major source of employment. There will be agents to help you choose your pension, your career, a new car, a healthy-living programme, what to learn and how to study, the colours in your new home – and even your image!

Many existing jobs will be transformed. Increasingly for example, doctors don't tell you what treatment to have. Patients come with all sorts of information about their condition gleaned from the Internet, magazines, self-help groups and other sources. Many don't want to be told what to do. They want help to choose between a variety of options. The doctor becomes an advisor – a consultant in the business sense of the word.

Many other occupations will take on this consultancy role, helping clients to choose. Instead of providing a one-size-fits-all service, professionals and others will have to come alongside the people they serve and tailor their response to each person. Agents will help organisations personalise their offerings.

Trusted agents?

But will we trust these agents? Most agents are producer con-
trolled, and consumers have become distrustful. Whose side are
the agents on? When the doctor advises a particular medica-
tion, is that because it really is the best or because, under pressure to cut costs, it is the cheapest? When a financial advisor
recommends that mortgage, is it because it is the best for me or
because the advisor is on commission?

Consumers will want agents who give impartial advice, who
are on their side. But if consumer power kicks in, producers will
kick back. They will fear that if they lose control, agents will
recommend a competitor. So we could see quite a tussle, consumers trying to wrest agents away from producers while the
latter hang on tight. Perhaps H. G. Wells got it wrong: the
future won't see a war of the worlds, but a war of the agents!

A spiritual agent

One of our colleagues in the Tomorrow Project, a bright man
in his mid-twenties, was describing some work he was doing on
the role of agents in the insurance industry.

When he'd finished, I said, 'If I put on my minister's hat,
that's the role I think churches should play. Church should be
an agent, helping people to steer through life. Every week you
would get help in deciding how to plan your career, or how to
decide what school to send your child to, or how to take out a
pension (not what pension plan, but what you need to think
about), or how to prioritise your spending, and all your other
day-to-day choices. You wouldn't be told what to do, but you
would be advised how to think about it, what considerations to
take into account and what Christian principles apply.

'For example, drawing on the expertise of lay people, a
sermon might comprise an interview with an educationalist
about schools in the area, how to find more information and
what issues parents might consider when selecting a school.

The minister might sign off the interview with a reflection on Christian values that should inform a school's ethos. If the educationalist didn't normally go to church, being listened to and welcomed might be a first step to regular attendance. Some churches do elements of this now and get a good response.'

The young man replied, 'Mike, you don't know this, but my parents never went to church, I've got no church experience at all, but if there was a church near me, with my kind of people [shades of 'it must fit me exactly'?] and it was doing what you describe, I might well go every week.'

Church could be a much valued agent in the emerging world. Church centres which provide counselling, advice and other services to their community are blazing a trail. But how many churches see managing choice as central to their mission?

Brands – the new Bible

Organisations will also use brands, as now, to help people to manage choice. Brands are products, magazines, celebrities and TV programmes that gain wide currency. They embody values and associations which people identify with. That helps them to choose one product over another. 'I trust this particular brand. That's what I'll buy. I won't give it another thought.'

The unboxing of people

Brands will grow in importance because people are leaving the old traditions behind. There was a time when values derived mainly from birth and upbringing. You were born into the traditions of your country, class, church, neighbourhood and family. Tradition, 'the way we do things round here', guided people's behaviour and outlook.

That has now changed for many people. Greater affuence has given birth to more consumer products, which have widened choice. The expansion of higher education has stretched the horizons of vastly more people, exposing them to new beliefs and possibilities. The spread of the Internet has spawned a plethora of interest groups, providing more opportunities to join different groups with different values.

These trends will continue, enabling more and more people to choose between different values rather than taking for granted those they inherited. Lifestyles increasingly will be chosen rather than given. Gone is the aim of keeping up with the Joneses: life is about being different to the Joneses, 'being myself'. To be authentic, one's own person, has become the great goal – and will remain so.

Discovering your routes

As more people are released from the old traditions, they will want help to choose from the plenitude of possibilities before them. John Grant, a marketing guru, argues that brands are emerging as the new signposts to life.[1] They are becoming ideas that guide individuals and shape their lives. Brands are the new traditions.

They lead people into new behaviours by arousing their interest. IKEA's 'Chuck Out Your Chintz' advertising campaign in Britain challenged people's taste and changed the 'decor culture' (nearly doubling IKEA's sales in the process). Theme cafes, such as internet and bookshop cafes, are giving pub culture a run for its money.

Brands validate people's choices. 'I would like to dress comfortably in a way that makes me feel young', thinks the sixty-year-old. As she reads the Sunday magazine, she sees pictures of her age group in track suits and imagines herself the same. 'The career woman', used in all sorts of promotional campaigns, validates the mother's decision to return to work.

When people shop around for clothes, holidays, furnishings and other consumer products, they answer the question: 'Who am I for other people?' Ideas associated with brands become a source of identity – 'girl power', 'the sloane ranger', 'middle youth'. Brands become guides to who you are. They have displaced church, and there is no sign of this being reversed.

Princess Diana, the brand

The late Diana, Princess of Wales, displayed many of the characteristics of a successful brand. She was:

A symbol, highly visible and widely recognised.

A celebrity whom the ordinary punter could identify with, feel close to and trust. She was not a flawless heroine, as with celebrities of old, someone whose example we should follow. She was an 'intimate celebrity'.

A creature of the media. She went direct to the people by using the media, bypassing formal channels. This enabled millions of people to think that they each had some sort of relationship with her.

A means of bringing people together. When thousands of people brought flowers and messages to Kensington Gardens after her death, the mourners were communicating with each other. The messages were to be read by thousands of other people passing by. 'It was like posting a message on a bulletin board on the Internet.' It was a way of saying, 'I'm part of this too.'

All successful brands share these characteristics. They are widely recognised, are often promoted by celebrities whom ordinary people can identify with, are dependent on the media and bring people together: frequently part of the motive for going to a film, or buying certain clothes, or selecting a particular style of kitchen is to say that I am doing this too, I am one of you.[2]

Branding the church

So how might church fight back? If St Paul could be a Jew to reach the Jews and a Gentile to reach the Gentiles, should not the church become a brand to reach people who are guided by brands – entering today's culture to transform it?

Some people would recoil at the thought. The last thing the church should do, they would say, is to allow itself to be trapped by the language and practices of marketing. The 'customer' might end up setting the church's agenda rather than God. The church would be recreated in the image of the market, the body no longer of Christ but of capitalism.

Yet marketing is not all bad. It contains the notion of service – identifying people's needs and meeting them. That is a very Christian concept. Of course distinguishing between 'perceived' and 'real' needs is crucial, and church will not want to pander to needs that are selfish, over-materialistic and unbiblical and which leave the poor to one side. Equally, it will not want to ignore lessons from marketing that can help it to meet genuine needs such as the desire to find meaning.

Learning from brands may help the church to perform the function of a brand – to help people find a path through life by providing a source of identity and promoting values to live by. But it will do this in a way that remains faithful to the gospel. What lessons, then, can the church learn from brands?

From hero to friend

Key to a brand's success is to persuade people that others they identify with are using it. That's one of the purposes of advertising. Yesterday's commercials used 'perfect' celebrities to achieve this. Celebrities were held up as intrepid explorers, ingenious discoverers and inspired performers, people to be admired for feats that the ordinary person could never emulate and so whose advice should be followed.

But nowadays people don't look up to others, they look sideways to people like them – and today's commercials reflect that. They rely on intimate celebrities – famous people that the ordinary person can feel close to. Nike portrays Ronaldo kicking a football round the beach with his children. The viewer thinks, 'Just like me. He's my kind of person.' Brands are 'cosying up' to people.[3]

There are important questions here for the church. Do

people say about a minister for example, 'She's my kind of person'? Does church present itself more like a spiritual and moral hero than a friend – 'We've found the answer, got our lives together, know how to be good', which is all very intimidating for those who are less sure? How many members of a congregation are honest about their failures and struggles, making it easier for 'ordinary' people to identify with church? In short, how close is the church to 'ordinary' people?

Church for people like me

Another secret of a brand's success is to create a sense of belonging. A thirty-year-old enters a room wearing the same designer label as someone else. They don't know each other, but instantly they feel they have something in common. They belong to the same tribe. 'She's my sort of person'. It's not what you like that's important, it is who you are like.

To compete effectively with brands the church must take seriously this desire to identify with people using the brand – to think instantly, 'They are my kind of person.' How many non-churchgoers visiting a congregation could say, 'They're just like me'? People will be more likely to join church if they can identify with others who belong.

So why not take church to groups of people who feel comfortable with each other? If you have got a group who enjoy being with each other, then one barrier to church will have been knocked down already. The problem of belonging will be out of the way, leaving you free to tackle the question of belief.

The Furnival in Sheffield, England emerged from a vandalised pub which has been fitted out to become a skills centre for young people, a training kitchen and cafe, with surrounding buildings earmarked for a launderette and multi-agency health and advice centre.

Worship and prayer is at the heart of The Furnival, but people are not invited to 'come to church' to find God's love and acceptance. Rather they are touched by Christ's grace as they work for

wholeness in the community through various projects and initia-
tives. Local people can see that this is church for them because it
is at the heart of their community – they don't feel they have to go
to someone else's church, and so they are beginning to identify
with it.[4]

The crowd controls

Strong brands draw close to people, they enable you to identify
with others and – above all – they are recommended by friends.
The 'golden arches' for example are highly accessible to ordinary people; they are clearly pro-family so that parents can
identify with others who are family-minded, but most important every child has friends who enjoy eating there. 'Can I have
my birthday party in McDonalds, Mum, like Jo?'

Word of mouth is vital to a brand's success because people
manage choice by following friends. 'She said it was a great film,
let's go!' 'All my friends think it's a cool label, I'd better buy one
too.' 'I know big business is out to con me, but if Jeremy says
it's OK, he's a mate so it must be alright.'

Following the crowd will become even more important. A
faster, faster world will leave less time to research alternatives.
A more complex world will leave people gasping for certainty.
More choice will leave people overwhelmed. The advice of
friends will save making enquiries, will provide reassurance
('She tried it and it worked') and will enable choice to be
avoided altogether ('I'll go with the flow').

Not for nothing has the emerging world been described as the
'network society'.[5] Networks of friends will be crucial – the
better your networks, the better your choices.

Bad news travels quickly

In 1999 Jayne Ozanne, a market researcher, convened some
focus groups to explore people's attitude to the Church of
England. She asked one group of teenagers to draw what
church meant for them. They were uniformly negative. One lad

drew a cage with a lion inside. 'That's what church does to you', he explained, 'it draws you inside and eats you up.'

Where had he and the others got their views about church from? It was clear from another exercise that it was not the media. The media these youngsters watched and read did not feature church. Their views came from the comments of people they knew who had actually been to church – perhaps for a wedding or funeral, possibly more often.

If the local church wants to be well regarded, it must work hard to protect its reputation. Everyone who has any contact with church must leave feeling satisfied. If families come to a wedding, why not give the children a book or a quiet game to occupy them during the less interesting parts of the service? If children leave church having had a good time, they will tell several of their friends and each friend may tell someone else. Church itself may become their friend.

Church – a failed brand?

Organisations will continue to help people manage choice by turning products into brands that guide people through life. To do this they will develop intimate brands that draw close to people, they will link individuals together (because they have the brand in common) and they will get them talking about the brand.

Is church a brand that people can feel near to? Do others like them belong to church? What do people who have had contact with church say about their experience behind its back? What would church have to do to become a strong brand that helped people to manage their choices?

Drilling down

Realising that people are swamped by choice, some companies are starting to make life easier. Firms like Proctor and Gamble are working with selected groups of customers to develop products that suit their needs exactly. If 80% of your products are bought by 20% of your customers, why not focus on that 20%, reduce the variety on offer, and give them exactly what they want at a lower price? You can always establish a separate company to cater for the other 80%, providing greater choice if they are willing to pay for it.

Unilever, home to Bird's Eye, Walls, Ben and Jerry's and countless other brands, is slashing its 1,600 brands to a core of 400. No doubt these will be marketed like crazy across the globe and continually refined to match consumer tastes. Instead of expanding choice to give customers exactly what they want, researchers will drill down to identify customer preferences more precisely. Choice will be exchanged for a tighter fit.

As more companies adopt this approach, people will assume that their wants have been carefully researched. They will have little time for organisations which have not done their homework. This will influence their expectations of church. Fortunately congregational audits, community surveys and other forms of research are spreading rapidly, helping churches to listen to people.

The listening church

Researching people you want to reach will not only aid evangelism, it will be a mark of respect, a sign that church takes people seriously enough to pay attention to them. This will help congregations to be more responsive to people. Often the church is very presumptuous. 'We know what will suit you. We have a package – a way of doing things – that's just right. Come and join us!'

If we took more time to listen we might discover that non-churchgoers do not share our confidence. Many cringe at our 'happy clappy' worship, or find our more formal liturgies wordy and dull. They do not trust church because church does not appear to understand them. If we were to listen to non-churchgoers, we might get some helpful surprises.

One church in Leicestershire, England asked families what time they would prefer their Sunday service. To its amazement, there was a large vote in favour of late Sunday afternoon – a time that is also becoming popular in Australia. Shifting the morning service to this new time has helped the congregation to grow.

A listening church will draw close to people. This will help to rebuild trust, which will make people more willing to seek the church's advice. Individuals will have enough confidence to turn to church when faced by their latest choice crunch.

New marketing, new morality?

Researching customers to give them exactly what they want could be tomorrow's megatrend. One day it may even reverse the relentless, post-war expansion of choice. When people were treated in a standardised way, it was natural that they should clamour for choice to express their individuality. The right to choose became the people's ethic. In the abortion debate for example the woman's right to choose has swung the popular argument.

But as we speed into a surfeit of choice, values may change. 'Don't give me more choice', we'll think as we enter a shop, 'just give me what I want'. 'I want what I want' will be the new cry. Getting on a plate exactly what you desire may replace choice as the preferred route to fulfilment. The right to choose may give way to a new ethic – the right to be satisfied.

'Satisfy me! Satisfy me!' Consumers will throw down the gauntlet. Any organisation wishing to grab people's attention will have to respond.

Satisfied by satisfaction?

Christians will have mixed feelings about this new morality. On the one hand, the right to be satisfied resonates with Christ's promise of fullness of life. On the other, satisfaction that is based on self-satisfaction leaves little room for compassion and service. Will Britain for example become cruel Britannia?

The people's choice?

So as organisations develop a more personalised relationship with their users, they are also helping them to manage choice. They are becoming the new gurus – people's guide to life. They will increasingly do this through the use of agents, by turning brands into 'the new traditions' and by researching their customers – all of which will draw organisations closer to people and help them to personalise their offerings. Whether organisations use their position to exploit people or benefit them will be a major Christian concern.

So too will be how the church responds. Will the church learn to connect with people's everyday concerns, providing practical help in making day-to-day choices? Will it become an attractive brand in its own right, one that people trust for advice? Will the church listen carefully to people and learn to understand them? Will the church in short draw alongside people and respond flexibly to different groups – 'We'll come to you on your terms' perhaps, rather than 'You come to us on ours'?

In the emerging it-must-fit-me world, if the church remains distant and standardised, unable to fit the people it seeks to reach, it will be ignored. Why not become a genuine friend instead?

Notes

1 John Grant, *The New Marketing Manifesto*, Orion, 1999.
2 Charles Leadbeater, *Living on Thin Air,* Penguin, 1999, pp. 18–27.
3 *Ibid.* p. 23.
4 Stuart Murray and Anne Wilkinson-Hayes, *Hope from the Margins. New Ways of Being Church*, Grove Books, 2000, p. 9.
5 e.g. Manuel Castells, *The Rise of the Network Society*, Blackwell, 1996.

CHAPTER FOUR

THE TWO-FACED SOCIETY

As we race to the hyperchoice world with 'it must fit me exactly' and 'I want what I want', many will recoil at the selfishness round the corner. But that is not the whole story. Society has a split personality – the values of the consumer and the workplace are poles apart.[1] Might some of these workplace values temper the selfishness of consumerism? And how might evangelism engage with this divided world?

The consumer mindset

When people put on their consumer hats, they adopt certain values and think in a particular way – about truth for example.

Truth is what I think it is

Traditionally people believed that there were objective truths 'out there'. We might disagree about what they were, but we had no doubt they existed. This began to change radically under mass society. People were flooded with options thanks to more consumer products, more alternatives to the old traditions and more exposure to different values through the media, education and travel.

Overwhelmed by alternatives, people felt that truth was less fixed and certain. Truth came to be seen as a matter of opinion, and tolerance was highly valued – 'It's up to you'. People should be free to choose between the possibilities. 'It's fine for you to be a Muslim, so long as you respect my right to be a Buddhist'.

As mass customisation transforms the global economy, this subjective view of truth will become more deeply entrenched. Consumers will not only select from alternatives to part-design what they buy (selecting from patterns and materials for example to order clothes that will suit them perfectly), they will do the same with truth. They will cherry-pick ideas to compile their own versions of what is true and false.

This will transform the understanding of tolerance. Even now as pick-and-mix becomes a way of life for younger people, tolerance is being redefined as the freedom not to choose between alternatives, but to combine them.[2] 'Why can't I be a Muslim *and* do some Buddhist-style meditation?' – a mosaic approach to life.

Three generations – true or false?

The boomer generation (born 1946–1960): 'Individualism and self-expression were important – they have been in a continual process of self-examination and in many ways can be described as a Peter Pan generation – never having completely grown up, or having left their youthful idealism behind. Their children sometimes complain that they have to spend a lot of their time supporting their parents through their emotional crises.'

Generation X (born 1961–1977): 'Individuality has been redefined by Generation X, because they feel no sense of the collective. Individuality is about protecting yourself from vulnerability and possible loss. Individuality is important because "you" are the only part of the world over which you have any control, "you" are the only one in whom you can trust. Where boomers focused on developing the self and acquiring things as an expression of that self, this generation seeks to protect the "self".'

Generation Y (born post-1978). 'This generation also refuses to be boxed in. Generation X disliked the way they were defined, but saw it as a sign of difference. The upcoming generation cannot think in that way – most of their remarks are prefaced by a personal caveat "Well, I can't speak for anyone else, but for me . . ." Not for them the surly isolation of the early stage of Generation X, nor the learnt political correctness of the Boomers – there appears to be a genuine assumption of individuality and tolerance. The language may sound the same, but there does seem to be a real difference . . . Whereas earlier generations have wanted more, it was usually a matter of making a choice; now it seems that you can be all things at all times . . . Identity is now a fluid concept – you are all the people you want to be.'[3]

Fun worship

The sociologist, David Harvey, has described how we are shifting from a society dominated by ethics to one dominated by aesthetics.[4] By that he means that people used to have a strong sense of moral obligation. This is giving way to a culture in which more than ever before people are driven by pleasure. Day after day the media presents endless ways to have fun.

Increasingly, as is already starting to happen, pleasure products will be tailor-made – such as a holiday constructed round me, or my own personal training programme or bespoke experiences. Our notion of what is pleasurable will become more demanding. It will be fun only if it suits me exactly.

Looking good to feel good

We have just left behind a century fascinated by what lay beneath the surface. It was the century of Freud and psychoanalysis, of probing hidden thoughts and memories, of distrusting what is conscious because it may disguise what is unconscious.

Mass consumption undermined this by teaching us to focus

on appearances, to prize what is attractively packaged and to be impressed by people who are well turned out. Appearance became the yardstick by which others were judged. A university student with spots on her face complained, 'Why do my friends judge me by how I look and not by how I am on the inside?'

In the it-must-fit-me world, immense strides in cosmetic surgery and other medical advances will hugely expand the opportunities for people to change how they look. People will be able to delay balding and other physical symptoms of old age. As they choose their appearance like never before, they won't always want to look perfect. They may prefer to look authentic. Some Americans are having their teeth put at a slight angle to avoid displaying perfect mouths like everyone else. They want to be unique.

More people's looks will be made to measure. They will buy clothes that are 'cut from a different cloth' or (in another commercial) a watch that is 'no ordinary old timer'.

The individual rules

Authority figures used to be held in respect and were entitled to speak on behalf of particular groups – a trade union leader perhaps, or the city mayor, or the Archbishop of Canterbury. People listened to their views because they represented the group, and the group mattered. It was a source of values.

Mass consumption, with its explosion of choice, has weakened the group. People now think in terms of personal autonomy. Individuals decide their values, not the group and its leaders. Individuals no longer doff their caps at authority. People are certainly influenced by others, but it is the individual who determines which consumer tribe to take notice of. 'Think for yourself', a clothing company advertised.

The 'it must fit me exactly' mentality will stretch this further. People will continue to belong, as now, to clubs, self-help groups and a whole variety of networks. But they will want to associate with people who fit them – not always because they are like them, but because they share an interest or get on well together. Individuals will not have the patience to resolve conflict and argument. 'Stick at it and make it work' will be a strange idea. If the group no longer works for them, they will search for a new one.

Fragmented selves

The expansion of consumer choice has allowed people to live richer and more varied lives. They can develop their spirituality by meditating once a week; they can express their moral concern by supporting Friends of the Earth; they can attend a weekly bridge club to make friends; they can go to the gym on Saturday and spend Sunday with the children. At each activity they will meet different people.

So they can behave differently on each occasion and no one will know. They can be deeply concerned about the environment at a Greenpeace meeting, and give it not a thought when they go shopping with the children. They may be health-conscious in the gym, but 'pig out' unhealthily with their bridge-playing friends. For many people, the self is fragmenting into different parts which behave inconsistently.

In an interview for *Newsweek* magazine in 1997, Bob Dylan was quoted as saying, 'I don't think I'm tangible to myself. I mean, I think one thing today and I think another thing tomorrow. I change during the course of a day. I wake and I'm one person, and when I go to sleep I know for certain I'm somebody else. I don't know *who* I am most of the time. It doesn't even matter to me.'[5]

The fragmentation of self is likely to increase as the Internet becomes more widely used. Even now a man may enter a chatroom on-line and present himself as a woman, a heterosexual as homosexual, a black person as white or a disabled person as someone without physical impairment.

With more people getting connected, experiments with different parts of the self will multiply. Someone who is placid in real life may try out their aggression in the virtual world. Will the opportunities to experiment diminish with improved visual communication on-line, or will people still value the Net's anonymity for some interactions?

The sun never sets on television

Over the last thirty years consumer culture has become highly visual, which has encouraged people to think in less logical, linear ways. Book culture promoted sequential thinking. You start at the beginning of the book and work logically to the end, paragraph by paragraph.

Thanks to television and now the new media, life has become packed with images. Magazines are crammed with pictures, computer software relies on icons. On MTV there is no overall story but a succession of images that viewers can use to create their own stories. Images foster intuitive rather than rational modes of thought, impressions rather than logic, thinking in parallel rather than in sequence, pictures rather than paragraphs.

As virtual reality comes on stream and the 'experience economy' booms, this new way of thinking will become more deeply embedded. 'Screenagers' will not only be bombarded by images, they will be immersed in one experience after another. Experiential icons will be the norm.

Workplace values

So much for the consumer world – a familiar picture perhaps. But people are not only consumers. They spend much time at work, or being educated for work or seeking it. When they enter the 'workplace' (including education), they take off their consumer hats and put on a very different set of values.

Consumer and workplace values

The consumer view	The workplace view
Subjective truth	Objective truth
Pleasure counts	Morality matters
Appearance is all	Substance counts
The individual rules	Teamwork is vital
The fragmented self	The consistent self
Pictures	Paragraphs

The bottom line

In the workplace, truth is not purely subjective. There are absolute values such as the need to make a profit, the rules of the market and the desire to succeed. There is a bottom line – and it will get thicker.

With the world interlocking ever more tightly, best practice will shoot from one part of the globe to another. If that is the best way to do it in Los Angeles, we will follow suit in Auckland. More environmental, financial and other regulations will be subject to international agreement. Workplace values will be globalised – a trend towards the objective rather than subjective.

Values add value

Morality is important at work, reflected for example in codes of conduct, equal opportunities policies, rules about sexual harassment, grievance procedures, business ethics and the incorporation of ethical values in many brands. As the global economy intensifies competition, distinctive ethical values will give companies a competitive advantage – by selling for example 'GM-free', 'fair trade' and other such products.

Quality pays

Though appearance will still be important in packaging and marketing, the quality of the substance – what lies within the

Some professions continue to struggle with quality control.

package – will remain vital. Quality control is a top priority for the food industry and for many others. With mounting global competition, no firm will dare risk their reputation through poor quality. Appearances will not be enough.

Profitable relationships

Teamwork and good personal relationships will become ever more necessary. Technology automates routine tasks and makes possible more complicated ones. These complex tasks are frequently beyond the skills of any one person, which is why we are hearing so much about teams, collaboration and inter-personal skills at work. 'Sorry, you'll have to call later. He's in a meeting.'

One study found that over a five-year period in the mid-

1990s, the amount of time spent relating to other people increased for a whole range of different jobs.[6] As technology continues to revolutionise the workplace, firms with good relationships will leap ahead.

Building a reputation

Consistency of behaviour will be increasingly valued, even though the multiplication of tasks and teams will create more opportunities for individuals to behave differently, with different groups of people, from one day to the next. With workers speeding from job to job and task to task, building a reputation will become the passport to steady employment. This will require a consistent track record. On the Net you can afford to be a woman one day and a man the next, but you can't get away with that at work!

Paragraph thinking

Although picture-based thinking is the norm for consumers and producing images creates many jobs, traditional patterns of thought will remain central to the workplace. The business plan, the financial statement, the supply chain (a sequential notion if there ever was!), reports and written contracts will all put a premium on logical, linear thought. Paragraph thinking will thrive for some years to come.

A culture-clash?

So people will live within two contrasting sets of values, one shaped by consumerism ('I want') and the other by the workplace which serves. Are these 'I want' and 'I serve' values incompatible with each other? They certainly depend on one another. 'I want' demands will be satisfied by organisations which serve. Contributing to organisations which serve will provide individuals with an income to spend as they want.

Individuals who occupy both realms, serving for much of

their time and satisfying personal longings for the rest, might seem to be living a balanced life. Might there be faint echoes of the Reign of God? Jesus taught an ethic of service, but also advocated a festive life. He likened the Kingdom to a banquet and enjoyed a thoroughly good meal himself. The first of his 'signs' in John's Gospel took place at a wedding party. Surely if service through work is balanced by pleasure, this is not so far from the Kingdom?

But of course it is not like that. Organisations may serve people in ways that reinforce selfishness rather than advance God's reign. In particular, many employees are so steeped in consumer values that they don't provide service willingly: they do it only because they have to. Nor do people find it easy to give up their individualism and become good team players. Nor again do they automatically behave ethically and consistently.

Persuading individuals to leave their consumer values outside the workplace door and embrace the employer's values will be ever more difficult. Regulations, codes of practice and contracts may become more detailed and prescriptive, with heavier penalties for failure to comply. Stronger financial incentives may be offered – you will be rewarded for your teamwork skills, as well as for completing the task.

Conditions of work will be individualised where possible, to compensate for the stress caused by squeezing consumers into a workplace mould. Work will take on a consumer veneer to make it more comfortable – management consultancy firm, Arthur Andersen, has involved the restauranteur, Conran, in the design of some of its London offices.

So although consumer and workplace values will need each other, these values will also be in tension – and managing that tension will be a major preoccupation. Will the workplace become steadily more consumerised – and if so, how will it cope?

Tearing the it-must-fit-me world apart?

It might be tempting to imagine that some of the workplace values are really those required by relationships, and to draw the contrast between consumerism and interpersonal ties. But many relationships take place within a consumerist framework, and will continue to do so. Home is an epicentre of consumerism.

More true is that consumer and workplace values also represent the two sides of personalised scale. Consumer values are emphasised when people want to be treated as individuals, whereas workplace values are essential if scale – organisations and networks – is to function properly. A small organisation will secure the benefits of scale only if it has the skills to collaborate with others. A large organisation will be inefficient if its internal relationships do not function well.

The tension between these values, therefore, is also a tension at the heart of the it-must-fit-me world. Scale is required to produce an ever-expanding range of personalised goods and services. These products in turn encourage an it-must-fit-me-exactly outlook that undermines cooperation within scale. Will these two sides of personalised scale pull so strongly apart that they become a major source of instability?

Evangelism in two worlds

To connect with the emerging society, church may have to take more seriously the two worlds that people inhabit. Although mission to these two worlds should involve much more than evangelism, what are the implications for communicating the gospel?

At work

At work, assumptions will persist that absolute truths do exist, that morality is important, that life is more than appearances –

the quality of the product is crucial – that relationships count, that consistency of behaviour matters and that to succeed you must be able to think in a traditional, book way. This will continue to create a mindset that is open to a particular style of evangelism – one based on rational presentations of the gospel.

'Here are some good reasons to believe. You know that there are some absolutes in the workplace, but which absolutes have eternal value? You know that morality is important, but who can help you to be a moral person? You know that appearances aren't everything, so who can change what you are like on the inside? Work relationships are hugely important for you, so how can you get on better with others? How can you be consistent with people and build a good reputation?' Presenting faith in a logical way will be in tune with the linear, sequential thinking that is essential for work.

Come back apologetics

Apologetics, traditionally the rational defence of Christianity, may have its most promising future within the workplace rather than outside. It will be able to tap into a set of assumptions that in some respects are friendly to the gospel. Of course there are many work values that are deeply hostile to Christian belief – the place of the money motive for one. But several key assumptions at work can form bridges into the gospel. In addition a logical, linear approach to evangelism may resonate with the style of thinking used at work.

This won't substitute for prayer, for the demonstration of Christ through people's lives, for bringing Kingdom values into the workplace, nor for evangelism built on healthy relationships. These are vital. But in addition, many people need persuading that Christianity makes sense, that the arguments in favour stack up, that you don't need an empty brain to believe. At this point, whether in one-to-one conversations or in more formal presentations, a logical defence of the gospel that makes connections with work can come into its own.

Spiritual training courses?

Evangelism based on training courses might be one vehicle for apologetics, and complement the personal witness of Christians at work. Courses on managing change or handling stress for example might present theory and best practice from the secular world, but conclude with an optional session. In it participants would be offered spiritual resources to help them apply what they had learnt. One couple are doing that in Britain with considerable success.[7]

Recently I visited Global Business Networks, a futures-based consultancy in San Francisco. I asked an experienced consultant what was the biggest challenge facing the organisations he worked with. Quick as a flash he replied, 'Trust.' Might that be an issue for training courses with a spiritual dimension?

The workplace is God's place

'We are being called on to look for common ground with non-Christians when, *in the workplace,* we already share it.

We are being exhorted to build bridges when, *in the workplace,* the bridges are already built and have been crossed.

We are exhorted to go and develop relationships with people but, *in the workplace,* the relationships already exist. We are encouraged to go out and fish in the pools and the puddles when we're sitting on a lake full of fish.'[8]

Among consumers

Consumers inhabit a very different world to work, a world populated by lifestyle tribes, a world that is generally less friendly to this rational approach. For consumers, truth is a matter of what I think, pleasure is more important than morality, appearance is everything, the individual rules, selves are often fragmented and people are immersed in images. This is less fertile ground for traditional apologetics because people are not thinking in a traditional way.

Emotions and sense experiences play a greater part. Consumers like to be titillated by taste, sights, smells, sound and how things feel. Instead of relying on logical presentations of the gospel, church is more likely to reach consumers by responding to their emotions and appealing to their senses – by creating a lifestyle bridge which is authentically Christian.

Eating till we burst

Parties, for example, are one of the icons of our age – birthday parties, leaving parties, Christmas parties, silver wedding celebrations, 'let's have an Indian together', tupperware parties (still) and many others. It is extraordinary the number of cafes and restaurants that exist. Many churches have found food to be an excellent contact point with consumer culture. Some have made eating an integral part of their Sunday evening worship.

The meal each time the course meets is one of the keys to the success of Alpha, a ten-week introduction to Christianity used all round the world. Eating together helps people to relax, make friends and feel they belong. Enquirers begin to experience Christian community before they assent to Christian belief. The gospel is certainly presented rationally, but in many cases it is the Alpha lifestyle, the whole experience that seems to be persuasive.

Evangelism tastes better with lasagne

Maybe a festive lifestyle will be one key to reaching consumers. Perhaps local churches should find ways of allowing people to grow into the gospel as they eat, drink, watch films and enjoy themselves in the company of Christians. Leaders may want to explore with enquirers ways of using pictures, music and items drawn from nature, for example, as aids to prayer. Teaching, involving video, sound-tracks and discussion, might be geared to helping people understand their everyday experiences of hope, disappointment and so on.

Drip-feeding the content of the gospel over a lengthy period will require patience and a delicate touch, a judicious knowing of what not to say and when to be more up-front. It may require letting the group evolve into its own distinct expression of church. Instead of the attitude, 'We've got so far, now let's get you into church', the leader might ask, 'Would you as a group like to explore what it means to be spiritual in your own particular way? As a Christian I'm willing to facilitate you, but it must be your journey.'

The 'Group' in Oxford, England has met on Thursday nights for over five years. They eat together in different homes, and punctuate the meal with a liturgy, songs, prayers and lots of laughter. They often discuss current affairs, and the relevance or otherwise of faith.[9] Admittedly they are mainly Christians, but might groups of non-churchgoers do something similar, allowing worship, prayer and study to evolve at the group's pace as it grows into faith?

Meeting in a pub is another way that some congregations have sought to be earthed in the consumer world. In the mid 1990s 'Cornerstone' was meeting in the 'Odd One Out', a pub run by Christian landlords in Colchester, UK. One of its leaders introduced it as 'open to all who are searching spiritually yet find conventional churches too daunting'.[10]

Right style, right place

The cultural canyon[11] between the workplace and the consumer creates new opportunities for church. It is not true, as some think, that apologetics has a vanishing role. It has huge potential – in the workplace. The trouble is that the local church is so disconnected from work that it has few opportunities to make its presence felt there. Might workplace congregations be an answer? ASDA in Liverpool opens half an hour later one morning a week so that its staff can attend a communion – in the store – first.[12]

Sadly many churches, seeking to reach people in their consumer lifestyles, persist with a rational mode of evangelism that is best suited to work – the traditional evangelistic sermon for instance. Though this can still touch non-believers, increasingly a mainly verbal presentation of the gospel feels out of place in the consumer world. Consumers are not in that frame of mind. They left logical, sequential thinking at work. They are into experiences and lifestyle. Reaching them may require an alternative approach – a festive life that remains true to the gospel but wraps it in a different package.

Becoming sensitive to the different mindsets of work and leisure would be a step away from a one-size-fits-all approach to evangelism. Church would have begun to leave standardisation behind; it would be reaching out to the it-must-fit-me world. Instead of dragging people at work to us, church would start going to them. It would be church that fits – not just those who've come in, but those who are currently outside.

Notes

1 Daniel Bell, *The Cultural Contradiction of Capitalism*, Heinemann, 1976 was possibly the first to explore this tension, but in rather different terms to what follows.

2 *Tribe – A Life of Change* (author unspecified), Barclays, 1999, p. 115.

3 *Tribe*, Barclays Life, 1999, pp. 100, 108–9, 115, 124. (*Tribe* reports the findings of market research into the cultures that are driving British society.)

4 David Harvey, *The Condition of Postmodernity: an inquiry into the origins of cultural change*, Cambridge, 1990, p. 321.

5 Eddie Gibbs, *ChurchNext*, IVP, 2000, pp. 25–6.

6 Francis Green *et al*, 'Are British workers getting more

skilled?' in A. B. Atkinson and John Hills (eds), *Exclusion, Employment and Opportunity*, London School of Economics, 1998.

7 See chapter 8 below.

8 Mark Greene, *Thank God it's Monday,* SU, 1994, p. 11.

9 Stuart Murray and Anne Wilkinson-Hayes, *Hope from the Margins. New Ways of Being Church*, Grove Books, 2000, pp. 12–13.

10 Stuart Murray, *Church Planting. Laying Foundations*, Paternoster, 1998, p. 162.

11 If we had time we could nuance this a little. For example there is a whole section of life, shopping for provisions, that falls somewhere between work and consumerism, embracing elements of both. See Daniel Miller, *A Theory of Shopping*, Polity, 1998.

12 Peter Brierley, *The Tide is Running Out*, Christian Research, 2000, p. 161.

CHAPTER FIVE

WHY CHURCHGOERS DON'T

It is not hard to imagine church in the West sprawled like a beached whale, eventually dying because it has been cut off from society. All that needs to happen is for congregations to persist with what they do now.

In the early '90s British churchgoers said, 'With the decade of evangelism, church decline is bound to be reversed.' In fact, during the '90s the rate of decline almost doubled. Even in the United States, where church is comparatively healthy, Christians cannot be complacent. The US is merely lagging behind the alarming trends in Britain. Unless we change our approach, overall numbers will continue to fall, church will become even more marooned from ordinary people and one day 'the vanishing church show' will disappear completely.

Society is being transformed. Everywhere we turn, change is in the air. Core to these changes is how organisations are relating to people in a more personalised way. Because this threatens option paralysis, organisations are also learning how to help people to manage choice – choice control is becoming central to people's lives.

At the same time, the emergence of the it-must-fit-me world is sharpening the divide between consumer and workplace values: people's lives are cut in two. These developments challenge the church to rethink how it relates to society in general, including how it carries out evangelism.

The situation therefore is even more dangerous than it might first appear. Not only has the church been losing ground for many years, it is now faced with the task of adapting to a new-look society. Can it rise to the challenge? To do so, it first needs to ask why numbers have been free-falling. Answering that will remove any thought that church can continue as it is.

Why the shrinking church?

There have been many explanations for why church is rushing to disappear. They can be grouped under three headings.[1]

Less belief, so less belonging

I recently took part in a television discussion in which two of the panellists argued that the church had no future. Christian beliefs were not plausible any more. One commented that she would like to return to the faith she once had, but she was still waiting to be persuaded. For these two, both academics, belonging to church was a matter of believing. First you believed and then you belonged.

This tends to be the approach of sociologists like Steve Bruce who claim that advanced society has become secularised.[2] It has become increasingly difficult for people to hold religious beliefs in a scientific age. Thanks to science, we take for granted rational explanations of the world based on observation. Belief in God fits uneasily with this. You can't put God under a microscope like you can a human gene.

Add the effects of consumerism and people end up with a shopping trolley approach to faith. They are surrounded by alternative religions and values. 'They can't all be right' is the response, 'so I'll just pick and choose what's right for me.' This weakens absolute commitment to any one set of beliefs, which eventually undermines commitment to any belief. 'If one belief is as good as another, why believe at all? Why not do without all of them?'

The result is that religious belief has fallen away, and this has led to a decline in church attendance. Why go to church if you don't believe? Less belief leads to less belonging.

Belief without belonging

This head first approach might appeal to certain academics and others, but is it the most helpful explanation of declining rolls? Not according to another sociologist, Grace Davie.[3] Using British and European data, she argues that the situation is altogether more complex. What we have is not less belief and so less belonging, but continued belief without belonging.

The decline in church attendance is not the whole story, says Davie. Churchgoing and religious belief have divorced. Many people hold traditional Christian views but never go to church, while others go to church but don't hold all the Christian beliefs. People who hardly ever step inside a church still believe in God, pray from time to time and hold values that resonate with Christian morality, while regular churchgoers not infrequently hold distinctly non-Christian views, such as belief in reincarnation.

The persistence of belief outside church, whether traditionally Christian or not, may provide fertile ground for the revival of faith, suggests Davie. Christians need to till this soil carefully by making belonging to church more attractive.

Less belonging, so less belief

A third sociologist, Professor Robin Gill,[4] has argued that it is not a case of less belief so less belonging, nor of belief without belonging, but of less belonging and so less belief. The decline in church attendance has come first: this has then produced a decline in faith.

Adults' religious views, Gill maintains, are greatly influenced by whether or not they went to church as children. For example,

Figure I
Some religious beliefs remain widespread

I do believe in . . .	1970s	1980s	1990s
		(percentages)	
God	74	72	67
Life after death	37	43	44
Devil	20	24	26
Reincarnation	24	26	25
Horoscopes	23	26	26
Foretelling future	48	54	47
Lucky charms	17	19	18
Ghosts	19	28	32
I don't believe in . . .			
God	15	18	27
Life after death	42	40	42
Devil	70	64	67
Reincarnation	53	57	59
Horoscopes	72	69	67
Foretelling future	41	40	46
Lucky charms	79	78	78
Ghosts	73	65	58

Based on: Robin Gill, *Churchgoing and Christian Ethics*, CUP, 1999, pp. 70–71.
Drawn from attitude surveys over the period.

according to one set of British data, non-churchgoing adults were more than three times as likely to believe in God if they attended church weekly in their childhood than if they did not. They were more likely to pray, to believe in heaven and hell, and to describe themselves as extremely or somewhat religious (see Figure 1).

In the light of this, the astonishing slump in Britain's Sunday school attendance (Figure 2) points to a radical de-faithing of British society. As fewer children have contact with church, generations will grow up with values that are ever more distant from traditional belief. The dwindling minority with a church

Figure 2
The proportion of children at Sunday school has fallen dramatically

Percentage of child population in Sunday school, UK, 1900–2000

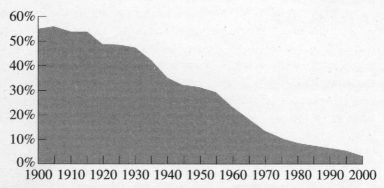

Source: UK Christian Handbook. Religious Trends 2000/2001. No. 2, Christian Research 1999

background will exert a shrinking influence. The same story will be told of Australia and New Zealand, and will be true even of the United States.

Grace Davie's evidence for persistent belief should be seen not as a sign of hope, therefore, but as residual belief that may decline further as church belonging recedes into distant memory. In 1999 MORI asked a sample of British people who were due to be eighteen in 2000, 'Do you have any religious beliefs?' A massive 77% said 'No'. For a growing number of people signs of faith appear to be occasional blips on an otherwise empty radar screen.

Why is church so unpopular?

The trouble with Robin Gill's argument is that he does not explain why churchgoing is now so unpopular. Is it part of a wider trend? Some people argue that individuals are becoming less willing to commit themselves to any group: they are more self-sufficient. So membership of trade unions, political parties and other organisations is in decline. Exodus from church reflects this shift from a joining to a stand-alone society.

Yet a number of organisations have increased their membership by leaps and bounds – Friends of the Earth and other environmental groups for example. Trend-spotter Faith Popcorn[5] has highlighted the upsurge of 'clanning' in the United States, including a revival of sewing circles, bridge clubs and roving poker games. Over half a million different kinds of support group are thought to meet in the USA.

People have not abandoned groups, they have fled particular types of group – and church is one of them. 'It's not my kind of thing.'

The disconnected church

This is largely because church is increasingly disconnected from people's networks – from their friends and workmates, and from shops, clubs, health clinics and other places they visit. 'My type of people don't go to church', which makes church the last organisation you would want to join.

Surveys[6] show that for most new Christians, conversion is a process that depends on the encouragement of friends and family. Non-believers dip a toe into church, they discover other people like them, they feel steadily more comfortable, and as their sense of belonging grows they become ready to make a commitment.

Once individuals find that 'my sort of people' are at church they are much more likely to attend. But if church is disconnected from people's networks, they will have little incentive to come along.

Disconnected from work

Church as an organisation is physically separated from people's jobs. Before the industrial revolution people usually worked from home or close to home, and church was just round the corner. But with the growth of towns, often homes ended up some distance from work. The commuting age began. Because churches were built near to where people lived, when people left home for work they also, in a physical sense, left the church behind.

The recent flood of women into paid employment has reinforced this enormously. Not only do men spend much of their time physically distant from home, but more and more women have been doing the same. This has sharply reduced women's involvement in their local communities, including church. In Britain for example, there was a 7% drop in women's interest in their local community between 1986 and 1996. The decline was most marked for women with jobs.[7]

Organised church has been left to minister to people at home but not at work, and so inevitably family-type issues dominate its thinking. When I became minister of a church in Somerset, England, I hoped that I would engage with people in their jobs as well as at home. But it was amazing how quickly work fell off my screen. I kept encountering people in their family setting – in weddings, funerals, home visits, family crises and the local schools, for example. I spent so much time on this that work scarcely got a look in. I became trapped by the domestic agenda.

This is true of so many ministers that it is hardly surprising faith and work have been wrenched apart. If church as an institution is largely absent from the workplace,[8] how can it address the concerns of work? Church feels irrelevant to what preoccupies the bulk of people's time.

Explaining the work/church divide

PhD researcher, Andy Jolley, asked 15 of Britain's faith and work 'experts' why they thought faith and work had been pulled apart. He categorised their responses as follows:

1. Many Christians act as if church was the 'be all and end all' of the kingdom of God.
2. Many Christians doubt that God is very interested in their work.
3. Lack of teaching on work and vocation in churches.
4. Full-time clergy dominate the church. So their agendas – which are church-focused – have priority over lay concerns.
5. Many clergy lack experience of work outside the church.
6. Churches are organised around the neighbourhood or parish. They are based on where people live and not where they work.
7. The industrial revolution dragged work away from church and home, providing a physical underpinning for the Enlightenment's intellectual spiritual/secular divide.[9]

Work – tomorrow's obsession?

This will become even more true as work looms larger for a growing proportion of the population. Already work has a tight grip on some people's lives because of the benefits it can bring. The hospital consultant, for instance, not only draws a good income, but has status within the medical profession and outside, derives purpose and achievement from the job, makes friends at work and has a sense of belonging – to a hospital community and a professional one.

For years, fulfilling jobs like this have been a small minority. More often the tedium of the assembly line, the scorching heat of a foundry, the dirt of a coal mine and the long hours behind the steering wheel made work a drudgery. The laughter of work-mates provided welcome relief, but the job itself brought little satisfaction. 'I can't wait to retire' was said with real feeling.

This has begun to change, and will continue to do so. Although many monotonous jobs will remain, technology will continue to automate routine tasks and make possible more complicated ones, which will require more skills and more collaboration. As jobs become more challenging, more people will seek fulfilment through work.

Ed Mayo, director of the New Economic Foundation, a

British lobbying group for a better environment and workplace, says 'Our surveys on quality of life show that the number-one concern now is people's desire for fulfilling work.' Michael Willmott, co-director of the Future Foundation, agrees. 'I am sure that work is becoming more important. People are getting at least as much sense of who they are from their work as from their family and friends.'[10]

David Cannon, author of *Generation X and the New Work Ethic,* argues that in North America and Europe the young graduates of today want work which is interesting and not just well paid. They will gravitate to organisations which offer them autonomy and project-based work rather than slotting them into a hierarchical career.[11] As higher education continues to expand,[12] these expectations will spread. People will want work to demonstrate their individuality, not to be boxed into a stereotype.

'Work's so important to me, so why's church not interested?'

Church will face a crisis. When work was drudgery, people sought fulfilment outside the job. Work was just a means to enjoy the rest of life. The home, the pub and possibly the church became centres of meaning and satisfaction. No one expected church to engage heavily with work. Church dealt with things that were ultimately significant, and work was not one of them. The tedium of work reflected the Fall, and not much more needed to be said.

However, as more people seek self-expression through work, the church's absence from the workplace will prove a growing missionary scandal. A crucial sphere of meaning, camaraderie and fulfilment, a sphere of growing significance to ever more people, will be outside the church's orbit.

Work will be at the centre of an expanding number of people's lives. Individuals will be wrestling with stress, ethical dilemmas, rapid change and the search for fulfilment, like sailors frantic to keep the ship afloat in a storm. Individual Christians may be alongside them, being church in how they conduct their personal lives. But organised church will be nowhere to be seen. Like Jonah, it will be asleep in the bottom of the hull.

If church is not involved in what really matters to people, why should they take any notice? Non-believers may be aware of colleagues who 'go to church', but – as now – this will be to some mysterious activity miles away. Evangelistic events will still be organised by the local church, and in suburbia especially Christians will continue to complain, 'But I can't invite anyone. I don't know people round here. If only I could invite my workmates, but they live miles away!'

Organised church will remain off the map – a map that matters to people. So non-believers won't give it a thought.

Disconnected from the consumer

In much of the advanced world, the decline in church attendance correlates well with the rise of consumerism. In Australia for instance, the spread of television after 1956 created the Sunday Night Movie which became the great draw card of the week. By the mid-1960s most churches had abandoned their Sunday evening services.

The 1950s boom in home ownership turned home-improvements and landscaping into a major preoccupation, competing with church. Later the liberalisation of Sunday trading permitted shops to open throughout the weekend, high car-ownership and cheap petrol transported people to the beach while Sunday became increasingly popular for children's sports, all of which clashed with church. Australia became known as the land of the long weekend, but somehow God didn't quite make it to the beach.

Consuming – the alternative to church

At the height of churchgoing, when roughly half the population or more attended church regularly, church was a source of identity – 'I'm Church of England', 'I go to the chapel'. It provided a framework for living through regular church services and social events, a network of friends, a means to feel better about yourself ('God accepts you unconditionally') and a source of meaning (church explained what life was for).

Today consumerism affords many of these benefits. Consumer lifestyles provide a source of identity – 'she likes the same music as me', 'we watch the same television programme', 'we wear the same designer labels'. Consuming structures our lives, such as the weekly trip to the gym, Saturday morning shopping and the much anticipated summer holiday abroad. Friendships are nurtured in the context of leisure – bowling together, drinking together or having a meal out. Consuming creates a sense of well-being – feeling good by looking good for example. Life acquires meaning as we spend in ways that will impress our friends ('I know all about wine.').

Church is failing to compete

Much of what the church can do, consumerism appears to do better. Looking good may boost people's self-esteem more immediately than the unconditional love of an invisible God. Therapists of all kind can provide a more tangible ego massage than a minister standing at the front of church. Consumer experiences can be every bit as powerful, and often more so, than spiritual experiences in church. Church music and decor seem unbelievably tame compared to dance culture.

Church is increasingly distant from the consumer world. If you want your back treated, you might look up the address of an osteopath. How many people would turn to a Christian healing centre? Would there be one close at hand? If you want to relax you might go to a sports centre, a restaurant or the cinema. Would you think of going to church? If you want excitement you might go bungee-jumping or save for an exotic holiday. How does church compare? If you want to stretch your mind you might enroll for an evening class. How many churches appear on an evening class programme? People flock to the supermarkets, but hardly anyone enters the average church.

However much Christians dislike competition, the truth is that the church is losing ground in the marketplace – and the pressure will mount as consumerism becomes more deeply entrenched and more sophisticated. Yet all is not lost. Church still has much to offer – a sense of meaning and hope, help with getting in touch with God, and friendships, for example. It needs to market these 'products' more effectively.

Disconnected from 'people like me'

When people were firmly embedded in their local communities, a newcomer to church would be likely to see people they knew. There would be a familiarity about the congregation.

Today, although people still identify strongly with where they live, with familiar landmarks such as the cinema, the supermarket or a street well travelled, increasingly they know people in the locality less well. Their friends are drawn from further afield. They still want to mix with people who are like-minded, but 'like-minded' are less often people from the same place or the same social background. 'Like-minded' are people who share common interests or who are easy to get on with. Communities of place are giving way to networks of interest.

The 'it must fit me exactly' mentality will reinforce this trend. People will network with those who share an interest, have a hobby in common or are involved with work. They will expect the network to be hassle-free – 'it must work for me. I can't be doing with all this conflict.' When it no longer fits, they will move on.

This will influence their attitude to church. Already the mindset is quite familiar: a teenager enters church, looks around, sees no one her own age. 'These aren't my sort of people.' She doesn't come back. A couple in their mid-twenties and living together reach the same conclusion. They don't

Our sort of people.

return either. The same happens for a single mum, a senior
bank executive or a disabled person.

'Now I understand why we won't grow'

Regular worshippers frequently rejoice in the mixture of people
at church. Their differences are bridged by their love of Christ.
But non-believers, peeping into church, do not share this love.
They need to find other things in common to be drawn in. Often
they can identify with only one or two people, if any, in the congregation. 'They're not my sort of people.' So they don't come
back.

I was talking about this to some church leaders. At the end
of the session one lady commented, wistfully, 'I come from a
village church. Thank you for explaining why, in human terms,
our church will never grow. We are not connected to the com-

muters, to the young people and to the other important networks in our village.'

As the it-must-fit-me-exactly mentality gets a stronger hold, churches which are not 'my sort of people' will struggle to survive.[13]

Taking 'top of the flops' off the air

The church has left the playing field. It has fled the workplace, consumerism and the networks where individuals find others like them – all that is important to people. At the very time that it needs to make new connections with the it-must-fit-me world, church stands in splendid isolation, offering a standardised 'you come to us' product that no longer touches people's everyday lives. Is it surprising that so few want to belong? But as fewer belong, fewer will believe.

Kensington Temple is one of the largest churches in Britain. One way that they reach people is by getting in touch with those who are new to London. They find out, for example, what media Filippinos read, and then they advertise, 'Are you new to London? Would you like some Filippino food and to meet other people from home? If so . . .' – and they provide details of a Filippino meal and a contact number. Those who attend are introduced to a variety of programmes which can draw them into church if they want.

Here is a church that is using lifestyle to reach consumers – and is bursting at the seams. It is adapting its approach to different groups of people, drawing alongside them, helping them to belong before they believe and making it easy for them to say, 'Church contains my sort of person'.

In twenty years' time will we look back and say, 'That was just an aberration, an exception to the pattern of decline which has persisted more or less unchecked'? Or is it an example of a better way of doing church – of drawing closer to people and connecting with them? Is it time to take 'top of the flops' church off the air and replace it with a better show?

Notes

1 This is a simplified version of the four categories suggested by Robin Gill, *Churchgoing and Christian Ethics*, CUP, 1999, ch. 3. Gill's second and third categories are quite similar, and I have treated them as one, using Grace Davie as the exemplar.

2 Steve Bruce, *Religion in the Modern World*, OUP, 1996.

3 Grace Davie, *Religion in Britain Since 1945: Believing Without Belonging*, Blackwell, 1994.

4 Robin Gill, *Churchgoing and Christian Ethics*, CUP, 1999 pp. 64ff.

5 Faith Popcorn, *Clicking*, Thorsons, 1997, pp. 65–78.

6 e.g. John Finney, *Finding Faith Today*, British and Foreign Bible Society, 1992.

7 Helen Wilkinson and Melanie Howard *et al*, *Tomorrow's Women*, Demos, 1997, pp. 41–2.

8 A major exception of course are industrial chaplains, university chaplains and others who seek to minister in the workplace, but for all their efforts they touch relatively few people. Industrial chaplains have not seen their task as building worshipping communities in the workplace.

9 Andy Jolley, 'Relating Faith to Work: Is the Church part of the solution, or part of the problem?', *Anvil*, 17 (2), 2000, pp. 87–93.

10 Quoted by Richard Reeves, *The Observer Magazine*, 23 July 2000, p. 22.

11 Cited by Helen Wilkinson and Geoff Mulgan, *Freedom's Children: Work, relationships and politics for 18–34 year olds in Britain today*, Demos, 1995, p. 44.

12 e.g. the UK government plans that by 2010 50% of those under 30 will have been through higher education, compared to around 30% of school leavers in the late '90s.

13 I am grateful to Peter Brierley for his observation that there is a huge mismatch between the church and Christians who have gone through a divorce, or are single or people who cohabit. Often they feel that 'people like me' are not in church, and so feel alienated from it.

CHAPTER SIX

'GOD REFUSED TO DIE!'

'God is dead' announced the front cover of *Time* magazine in the 1960s. Thirty years later the social commentator Paul Johnson observed that 'the most extraordinary thing about the twentieth century was the failure of God to die. God survived, flourished even.' What are the signs that God will flourish during the twenty-first century? Having just examined the dismal state of the advanced-world church, are there trends that will favour the task of evangelism and give us hope?

Growth under our noses

Church is certainly flourishing on the margins of Western society. In Australia migration has led to the growth of ethnic-based churches – Greek and Serbian Orthodox churches for instance, and Vietnamese, Irish and Italian Catholic churches. Non-white now outnumber white worshippers in inner London.[1] Walk through London's East End and you will see 'Amazing Grace Mini Mart', 'Signs and Wonders Hairstylists' and 'Redeem Travels'. Britain's largest church is the 6,000+ strong Kingsway International Christian Church in Hackney.

The lights are green for more of these churches to grow in future. Immigration to Britain over the past decade has been higher than expected, and official projections of the future trend have recently been raised – from 65,000 a year till 2016 to 95,000.[2] Britain's experience is not unique. Throughout the advanced world net immigration is likely to increase.

An immigration surge in the advanced world?

Shortages of labour in affluent societies could create a strong demand for immigration to plug the gap. These shortages will be due to:

Low fertility rates. Throughout the advanced world, not enough people are being born to replace those who die. If current trends persist and there is no increase in net immigration, in 100 years' time Europe's population will be half what it is today.

More young people in full-time higher education. For example, the proportion of under thirties in higher education is set to rise from around a third in 2000 to one half in 2010. Many will work part-time, but they will not be available for full-time jobs.

More people retiring than young people entering the workforce. Eventually older people may choose to work for longer, but it will take time for expectations about retirement to change.

Technology increases jobs. It does not reduce them – witness the recent job explosion in the USA. Technology creates wealth, more of which is being spent on high-employment services. (More people work in Britain's Indian restaurants than in shipbuilding, steel and coal-mining combined.) It generates a flood of new jobs, such as web-page designers. And it also makes possible more complex tasks, requiring people to spend more time working together which is labour intensive.

We are in a swing from job shortages as a major issue to people shortages. Will Europe and Australasia follow the United States in allowing immigration to be a solution? And will 'push' factors such as fewer job opportunities and political oppression in the two-thirds world fuel a steady stream of people willing to leave?

Coming from places where the church is well established and growing, many of these new arrivals will already be Christians. They will strengthen local churches among ethnic minorities. Booming ethnic churches will be an important part of the landscape. Will these churches remain on the edge of society, largely cut off from the mainstream? Or will they have the vision and confidence to reach out and help to revive traditional church? Will they be given a welcome if they do?

Open minds

What about mainstream society? What are the prospects for church there? One source of hope is that people are becoming more open to church.

Less hostility

When Christianity was dominant in the West, non-churchgoers often rejected the church deliberately and self-consciously. It was widely expected that people would go to church, and so if you chose not to you were under some pressure to give yourself – and others perhaps – a reason.

Reasons were not hard to find: church was boring, irrelevant, stifling and, in a scientific age, incredible. As the trickle of people leaving church in Europe and Australasia became a torrent, a culture of hostility towards Christianity emerged. People defined themselves against the church.

In much of the advanced world, however, the most recent generations have had little contact with church, so they do not feel the need to be against it as their parents were and they do not have the same hostility towards it. They are growing up in a 'post-modern' climate which assumes that 'Your beliefs are fine and so are mine'. In a climate which values tolerance, attacking the church feels unnecessary. This should make dialogue between Christians and non-believers easier in future. Non-churchgoers will not be on the defensive.

Fewer expectations

Possibly more important, they will have fewer preconceptions as to what church should be like. They will be more open to expressions of church which fit them – worship on weekdays rather than Sundays perhaps, and in styles which suit their taste. They will not be so suspicious of new forms of church, 'This isn't proper church. It's church just trying to impress me.'

The generations which left church had a clear idea of how church 'should be done'. Attempts to woo them back had to not only overcome the reasons why they left, but cope with their expectations of church. New music, liturgies and other changes meant that often evangelism was about inviting people back to a church which was very different to the one they had left.

Facing something different is frequently harder than facing something new. With something new you don't know what to expect, and so – as millions of visitors to Disneyworld can testify – you are more willing to take it on its own terms. But with something different, you have to go through an experience akin to bereavement, as you face the loss of what was familiar.

Visitors returning to church found that familiar hymns and words, frequently with childhood memories attached to them, were missing. As with any bereavement, many felt slightly bewildered, sensed that something important had been lost, wondered why it had gone and even felt angry about it. They were hardly in a state of mind to be persuaded to return!

Ready for church that's new

With the emerging generations the task should be easier. For the most part they have never been to church, so they will not expect church to be one thing and wonder why it has changed. They will avoid the ambivalence of those who actively left church – who disliked what it was when they left and then disliked the changes to make it better. They may be more open to church, provided it is real to them.

Might these new generations inspire a fresh start? Because they have no expectations of church, might they find it easier to explore new expressions of church which are authentic to them? This would require existing churches to be responsive to them, and perhaps to allow novel forms of church that make some long-standing Christians anxious – 'Church on Monday morning in the workplace! What will happen to congregations in the suburbs?' But might the reward be a church that is in touch with the emerging world?

Spiritual revival

'Something extraordinary seems to be happening to the spiritual life of Britain', claim researchers David Hay and Kay Hunt.[3] Their first look at findings of the BBC's Soul of Britain survey in 2000 show that over 76% of the population admitted to having had a religious experience. This was up by 59% in just over a decade, and by more than 110% compared with 25 years before. Spirituality has not been snuffed out by consumerism: rather, it may have been heightened as the treadmill of 'spend, spend, spend' leaves people feeling empty inside.

There is plenty of anecdotal evidence to support this. For example, a number of British churches have started prayer visitation schemes. A letter may be sent to all the homes in a street, informing them that a couple from the church will be calling unless the occupants object. The pair make their visit and offer to pray for people in the home. Often the response is very positive, so much so that one church in Rochester, England now aims to visit every home in its area over three years. People may not go to church (or to the mosque or synagogue), but they do connect with prayer.

Mention religion today and there is not even a tiny bit of interest. But talk about spirituality, and that seems to press a button. There is a widespread desire to be part of a larger whole. (Perhaps that is one of the attractions of the Internet, as well as of ecology.) Though many people live from day to day, beneath the surface they long to find an ultimate meaning. People are interested in the supernatural if the subject is raised. 'There must be something out there.'

Will this interest in spirituality remain, as now, largely private, individualised and unfocused, or will it once more be channelled into church? Much may depend on whether we can move away from standardised church which requires newcomers to worship in a uniform way.

From standardised church to solo-spirituality?

In the past, standardised congregations required everyone to sit, stand and kneel at the same time. They were instructed what to think through the sermon, and it was expected that they would all believe roughly the same. People who did not fit the mould left. The evacuation of the church since the 1950s involved a flight from this uniform approach.

Some people have taken refuge in highly individualistic forms of spirituality, spirituality that is practised in groups of one. But it is not easy for spirituality to flourish when you are on your own. It can help to pray with other people, whether the prayers are formal, extempore or silent. A group in prayer creates an atmosphere which encourages each member to pray. Being with others aids worship too. As other people come into the presence of God, you are drawn along with them. Learning about the faith with others provides stimulation and encouragement.

The larger entity creates a context in which the individual can encounter God. Take away that context, and it becomes much harder to develop your spirituality. You can be more easily distracted, and you will lack the support and stimulation of others. While there is certainly a place for personal prayer and study, there is little future for solo-spirituality done purely on your own.

Or a more personalised church?

In the it-must-fit-me world, when scale will be used increasingly to tailor products to the individual, an approach that avoids these extremes may well find favour. Churches that combine the benefits of people being together with freedom for individuals to make their own spiritual journeys could prove attractive to those interested in spirituality. The it-must-fit-me-exactly mentality will not be at home in standardised church, but equally the realisation is likely to grow that solo-spirituality is a dead end: you can't get far alone. There could be a demand for something in-between.

Donald Miller at the University of Southern California spent five years studying Calvary Chapel, Vineyard Christian Fellowship and Hope Chapel, which are reinventing the way Christianity is experienced in America and attracting large numbers of people who are alienated from institutional religion.[4] He found in effect that one secret of their success was that they had begun to occupy this middle ground.

For example, they had a laid-back style of worship and valued strongly personal encounters with God. This afforded more scope than in traditional churches for people to make their own spiritual journeys. At the same time there was an overall framework to guide individuals, while the intensity of the corporate worship – made possible because people were together – heightened each person's experience of God.

Laid-back church

One sign of hope for the advanced world is that a number of growing churches are learning how to combine the advantages of a group experience with greater freedom for individuals to engage with God in their own way. So instead of the whole congregation saying the creed together, a time of reflective worship after the sermon provides space for individuals to have their own unique communications with God.

Contemporary worship songs tend to express the individual's response to God rather than proclaim the 'objective' theological truths of more traditional hymns. Instead of everyone standing to sing, it has become more common for worshippers to stand, sit or kneel as they wish. Truth is still preached, but the sermon is less declamatory, with PA systems allowing a more conversational approach. In 'charismatic' churches, prophecy and words of knowledge from the congregation undermine the notion that truth comes only from the minister.

Might teaching become more invitational and less prescriptive in future? A style that invites people to consider a truth is more likely to appeal to an it-must-fit-me world than one which tells them what to think. 'Here is something that Christians have traditionally believed, this is why we think it still makes sense, but what do you think? Make up your own mind. If you disagree, we'll still love you and you will still be welcome here.'

Use of pictures, poetry and visual objects for example will engage people's senses, helping those who prefer a less cognitive approach to find truth through their emotions. 'Tadpole Christianity', all head and no body, has little appeal nowadays. The search for personal experiences will encourage faith to be wrapped around the individual.

Few churches have fully made the transition to this more flexible, laid-back approach. But some have moved in this direction, and as more do so – and do so more completely – church may become more attractive to those who are 'into' spirituality and want to explore it further. Church may connect with our more spiritual age if it offers not only a spiritual map, but the freedom for people to select the route most helpful to them.

Churches will draw the map a little differently, some will offer more routes than others, but both creating the map and allowing people to find their own paths on it will be essential if church is to resource the emerging generations. There are signs that some churches are beginning to do this.

Back to Christianity?

But will people tuned to spirituality look to Christianity rather than to Islam or another faith? Probably 'Yes', if the church can become attractive, because Christianity has so much to offer. At the pressure points emerging in society, church can still be a matchmaker between divine love and human need. Moreover, Christianity has been part of the lifeblood of Western history. Reconnecting with church would recapture a distant memory, rather than involve people in something totally new and more risky.

So there is fertile ground for church to till. Widespread interest in spirituality, the advantages of exploring spirituality with other people, signs that some churches are learning how best to help people along their spiritual paths and the riches of the Christian faith – all this provides hope that spirituality will become a springboard into church.

Points of contact

There will be masses of opportunity for the church to make contact with people in the years ahead. For example, people have a great desire for togetherness. It is true that they are also highly individualistic. They see themselves as the source of values. They don't want to be told what to think or do. 'It's up to me'. But they also want to belong.

Longing to belong

Much of consumerism is done with others – eating and drinking together, going to a film with friends, watching a football match in the pub, talking about last night's TV programme and buying the same brands as people you identify with. Belonging is central to consuming. 'She goes to the same shops as me.'

As we rush towards tomorrow, 'brand identity will be about togetherness – the emotional market, which is about solidarity

Figure 3
The changing face of community

	force for change	
Traditional and local	⟵⟶	Freely chosen and non-local
	household fragmentation	
Family relations	⟵⟶	Extended family links (e.g. second families after divorce)
	effects of mobility	
Neighbours and networks of local friends	⟵⟶	Dispersed friends
	mobility/telecommunications	
Local organisations	⟵⟶	Dispersed communities of interest (e.g. on Internet)
	importance of networking	
Local workplaces	⟵⟶	Non-local workplaces (community of colleagues)

Source: Adapted from The Henley Centre, *Planning for Social Change*, 1996–97

and interpersonal relationships . . .', says Denmark's Rolf Jensen, strategic adviser to over 100 leading international companies. 'More and more companies will need to think about how their own brand identity can be focused on the idea of drawing people together.'[5]

The half-million plus different kinds of support group that are thought to meet in the USA include Alcoholics Anonymous, Alien Abduction Victims, Airplane Phobics, Artificial Limb Patients and Asthma Sufferers under the letter 'A' alone.[6] People still want groups.

This contains fabulous opportunities for evangelism. For community is at the heart of church. When someone joins church, hopefully they join a community where they will be loved, in which they can find a framework for life, which will help them nurture their spirituality and to which they can make a contribution, boosting their self-esteem. Church should be superbly placed to meet the longing to belong.

Church out of the box

But to do so the church will need to think more imaginatively about what it means to be a community. Joan was in her sixties, had recently moved home and then lost her husband. A friend asked her how she was getting on. 'I'm not lonely any more', she replied. 'I've joined a Rock 'n' Roll club. I go two or three times a week, and we're off to Memphis this summer as a group.' She had found a community where she could belong.

Imagine that a few Christians with a passion for evangelism and for Rock 'n' Roll had formed the club. They might have introduced a course on spirituality as an optional extra for members of the club. Might the club eventually have spawned a Rock 'n' Roll congregation? Joan could have found belonging in a church.

In the tailor-made world, individuals will increasingly seek others who fit them, flocking to groups with a common interest. One way to evangelise would be to build congregations around these shared interests. People would first belong to an interest group. Then, in the context of belonging, they might be given a chance to explore spirituality if they wished.

A graduate of the Church Army College in Sheffield has been appointed to work among the dance clubs in Bournemouth, England. Her ambition? To form a dance church. Why not more churches like that?

Opportunities among young people

There will be huge opportunities among young people. Not only are children often spiritually open, but parents – and society as a whole – are increasingly concerned about children's well-being. Will my child turn to drugs? How can we support children if their parents separate? In this climate, the church

Sunday school at St Tesco's.

can expect considerable backing for work with children, if it is of high quality.

There will be no shortage of openings – mentors for teenagers (the British government plans that every 16- to 19-year-old will have an advisor), after-school clubs to help children with their homework and parenting classes, not to mention children's activities while mums and dads shop. In one way or another, church has started to be involved in all these. The Salvation Army, for instance, has opened a Sunday school in a large British supermarket.

Why not run an after-school club explicitly on Christian lines; at the end of the session encourage the children to share something on their heart with one of their friends, show them how to pray about it, keep a record of answers to prayer, let the children become excited about these answers and allow the club gradually to evolve into a small congregation? One woman started down this path with very positive results.

Opportunities among uprooted people

As society becomes increasingly mobile, more people will be uprooted from their homes to complete their higher education and to start a new job. One sixth of Americans move home each year, mainly to chase jobs, and one third of 20- to 30-year-olds do so.[7] Europe is likely to follow suit, slowly. If you do not play a sport or join some other club, it can be difficult to make friends in a new place. Our towns and cities are full of lonely people.

So why not advertise cheaply-priced meals for people who are new in town, with an opportunity to meet other new arrivals, and organise an additional programme of walks, film visits and discussion groups? Those who feel over-stretched at work might explore work/life balance, including a discussion of what spiritual resources could help. If the latter struck a chord, the group might consider an entire series on spirituality.

After I had spoken about different forms of church, one church in an English cathedral town went away to consider how they could serve newcomers to their town. They saw this not only as a potential means of evangelism, but as an act of compassion toward 'the strangers in their midst'.[8]

Opportunities among older people

Across the advanced world, more people will be getting older in the next 20 years. As they approach middle age and retirement, many will look back over their lives and wonder what they have accomplished. Some may be disappointed with their families or at failing to achieve their ambitions at work. Others may feel that they have been successful, but question what it

was all for. 'I have been successful, but have I been significant?'
They may be open to church if it can help fill the emptiness in
their lives . . .

*One church in Wales conducted a geodemographic study of their
locality. Instead of setting up a church and asking if people
wanted to come, they thought they would discover what real needs
existed first. One of the results was a plan to plant a congregation in an old people's residential home. The residents will lead
it, there will be a Sunday service and the equivalent of house
groups will meet during the week. The church involved will
provide training, musicians and occasional inputs through testimonies.*

*This will be much more than a service for residents staged by
members of the local church, which happens in many places. It
will be fully-fledged church taking root within the residential
home, owned and run by the people there. As it becomes part of
the life-blood of the community, it is hoped that non-churchgoers
will begin to see it as their congregation and start to attend. The
aim is to revitalise the last stages of the residents' lives.*

These and countless other opportunities will need church to be
more flexible in how it approaches evangelism. Old strategies
may no longer work, new ones that go out to people and build
church round them may be required. Will churches be willing
to change?

A nimble church?

Foundations for change are being laid. In Australia the denominations have had to come to terms with what it means to be
Australian. Recently they have begun to jettison much of their
English heritage, and to write distinctively Australian liturgies
and songs for example – the carol 'Christmas in the scrub' talks
about the heat of Christmas rather than the bleak midwinter.

This is creating a mindset more sensitive to differences in culture, which could help the church to respond more flexibly to the diversity of people groups within Australia.

In Australasia and Britain leaders are aware that the church is close to collapse in some areas. Figures for church decline have underlined how serious the situation is overall. There is a new edge of realism, with leaders more willing to affirm emerging church as well as traditional church. This also reflects generational change. The large number of ministers ordained in the 1950s and '60s are retiring, while the smaller number replacing them are more critical of the status quo.

The Decade of Evangelism has brought a mental shift from maintenance to mission. But because many of the evangelistic methods used during the decade have not worked, there is a widespread feeling that something new is required. Might we be entering a period of experimentation? As we shall see, new models of church are beginning to emerge and they may point the way forward. Recent inspirations, such as the Alpha course, may adapt and develop to become new beacons as well.

The church has proved hugely adaptable over the years – look at the history of church music. Why should it stop changing now?

A turning tide?

The tide may be about to turn for the church, where it has been in decline. Over the next 20 years church will face less hostility. People are likely to remain interested in spirituality, many could welcome support for their spiritual quest, and as church becomes more laid-back it could be attractive to those who are seeking help. There will be plenty of opportunities for church to connect with people.

All this will require new forms of evangelism that are built around people in their everyday lives. Some in the mainsteam churches are ready for this, and help could possibly be at hand from bursting ethnic-based churches. But are there enough people with the vision, the time and energy, and the skills to make it happen? Might it be a case of too little, too late?

Notes

1 Peter Brierley, *The Tide is Running Out*, Christian Research, 2000, p. 139.
2 Richard Bate *et al* (eds), *On the move: The housing consequences of migration*, JRF, 2000.
3 David Hay and Kay Hunt, 'Is Britain's soul waking up?', *The Tablet*, 27 June 2000.
4 Donald E. Miller, *Reinventing American Protestantism*, University of California, 1997.
5 Rolf Jensen, *The Dream Society*, McGraw-Hill, 1999, p. 65.
6 Faith Popcorn, *Clicking*, Thorsons, 1997, p. 73.
7 David Smith, *Will Europe Work?*, Profile, 1999, p. 97.
8 *cf* Leviticus 19:33–4.

CHAPTER SEVEN

A TEMPLATE FOR 2020

In 1956 Richard Riet Woolley, Britain's Astronomer Royal, made a prediction, 'Space travel is utter bilge'. He is one of many who have found themselves embarrassed by their certainties about the future.

Getting a grip on the future

Some people have concluded that the future is unknowable and so thinking about it is a waste of time. But we all make assumptions about the future whether we like it or not: that tomorrow will be the same as today perhaps, or that there is nothing you can do to change the future. Planning ahead is one of the characteristics of modern society. So are there ways to think insightfully about the future without getting it spectacularly wrong?

Alternative futures

It is because the future is so complicated and uncertain that techniques have been developed to take the unpredictable into account. One technique is to use scenarios to construct alternative descriptions of what the future might be like. Scenarios are a sophisticated version of what individuals do in their daily lives. People are always asking 'What if?' and trying to imagine the answers. 'What would happen if we went shopping on Thursday evening rather than Saturday?' someone might ask. They then play out the possible results in their mind. Scenario-thinking is much the same.

My work involves developing scenarios for the future of people's lives in Britain. We select a number of questions that feel important for the future – 'What might happen to parenting?', for example – research trends that will influence the answer and then work with teams of experts to construct alternative possibilities.

Scenarios: a case history

A striking use of scenarios occurred during South Africa's transition to majority rule. In the early 1990s 22 people from across the political spectrum met over several weekends to discuss the country's future. The convenor told them, 'We're not going to discuss what you would like to happen, only what might happen.'

Sub-groups produced 30 stories about how the future might unfold over 20 years, and presented them to the others. During the presentation only two types of interruption were allowed, 'Why does that happen?' and 'What happens next?' If the presenter could not answer the question, they had to sit down – the story was no good. To be useful the scenarios had to be consistent, plausible and meaningful to an audience: what did people in South Africa need to think about?

Eventually the scenarios were whittled down to four. 'Ostrich' envisaged the De Klerk government sticking its head in the sand. 'Lame Duck' foresaw a prolonged transition led by a weak government, perhaps a coalition, which deterred investment. 'Icarus' anticipated a black government crashing the economy as it embarked on unsustainable public spending to meet its electoral promises. 'Flamingos' foresaw a coalition government encouraging the country's different groups to fly together at a pace the economy could afford.

The scenarios were presented to a variety of audiences. They crept into public debate, and from time to time provided a nonthreatening way for MPs and others to consider the future. They are credited with helping the left-wing of the ANC to realise that a crash public-spending programme might not work, and some in the Afrikaans community to see that encumbering the transition process with too many safeguards might produce a weak and ineffective government.[1]

New century, new church

A little time back I asked one of my students to work with me on a scenario for the church in 2020. We could have developed a scenario that projected current trends forward. In the British context this would have produced an extraordinarily depressing future. Using the most recent figures, less than 1% of the population would be attending Sunday church in 2020.

We might have developed a scenario that took account of the flowering of church among ethnic minorities. We might have projected forward immigration trends which are set to increase. More people would be coming into the country, many of them from Christian backgrounds. Since future migrants are likely to include highly skilled workers, this would strengthen church not only in poorer areas but among enclaves of middle-class people too. Indigenous church would continue to melt away, but around the edge would be large pockets of vitality.

The scenario we settled for was rather different.

'Nottingham in 2020'

I have just moved to Nottingham, England. It is September 2020 and I am looking for a church. So I speak into my palm-held digital assistant or perhaps my television set (voice-activation is common-place). I ask for a list of churches in Nottingham. What do I find? A smorgasbord of churches to fit every taste.

There are a couple of teenage congregations, one on a Thursday evening and one on a Sunday. There is a 'Praise

Party' congregation for eight- to eleven-year-olds on a Saturday morning, in the town centre, reflecting the new 'drop 'n' shop' trend – parents drop off their children in a kids club and go shopping without them. There is a church for the 20s and 30s age group, one for single parents and several for different groups of disabled people. They all have different styles of worship, appropriate for each group.

Fragments everywhere

There is a church for business people. They meet for worship at 7.30 on Monday mornings, and then scatter around Nottingham, the UK and abroad. But they keep in touch with each other during the week by the successor to email. They do Bible studies and pray together on-line, collecting messages from one another at various times of the day when their busy schedules allow. They have plenty of fellowship, even though it is not face-to-face.

Meetings which are face-to-face, including Monday worship, are highly prized and well attended precisely because people who know each other well seldom meet physically at other times. Parents encourage their children to attend the Praise Party or one of the teenage congregations.

There are many other kinds of church. There is one for people who like jazz, another for those who are into classical music and a third for those who listen to Radio One. There is a dance church, a congregation for people escaping alcohol and drug dependency, one for asylum-seekers and even a church for the supporters of Nottingham Forest football club.

Traditional church has not disappeared. St Michael's up the road is still going strong, with large services on a Sunday morning.

A number of the congregations are small, some are quite large and several are transient. The congregation for single parents, for instance, tends to be a staging post. Parents find mutual support by worshipping and fellowshipping together, but after a while individuals move to other congregations where there is a greater mixture of people. The twenties and thirties congregation is much the same. Its 2,000 worshippers are a megamagnet, drawing in many who are unchurched, but an equal number leave each year for congregations with a different style.

Joined-up church

It is a fragmented picture. But look more closely, and you will see that the fragments are interlinked. Various groups draw people from across the congregations, including groups using dance, drama and the visual arts in evangelism. Those with an interest in the healing ministry meet for training and mutual support every couple of months.

There is a Christian environmental group, one that coordinates emergency aid to natural disaster victims and another that works among homeless people. An extensive prayer network is based around neighbourhood cells: people from different congregations meet to pray for their street or group of streets. In the new network society no one belongs to just one network, and that is certainly true of the church.

Several large events draw people together. Vast celebrations – one 'catholic' style, another charismatic, a third teaching-based and a fourth using Taizé music – are held from time to time. Individuals meet members of other churches when they attend huge holiday weeks like Spring Harvest or New Wine (they still draw the crowds), when they go on pilgrimages (now a popular form of tourism) and when they attend the newly introduced 'harvest banquet' – a gigantic mid-September barbecue to which Nottingham churches invite the city: anyone can come, free of charge.

Digital prayer

A recent development has been made possible by the introduction of large flat television screens, which can be hung like immense drapes at the front of a church or on a wall. These

The new prayer ministry had not anticipated this response.

have been in the pipeline since the 1990s, they have been on sale since about 2010 (mainly for use in people's homes), and in the past few years they have become sufficiently cheap for many congregations to buy one. They have started to be used in worship – to show video clips during a sermon and to present animated versions of Scripture.

They allow congregations to pray for each other visually. When St Michael's prays for its teenagers, a video clip shows what is happening in the teenage congregations, including some of the worship and an interview with a lad who has just started to attend. St Michael's can then see what they are praying for. The teenagers, when they meet, see a clip of the new-style Alpha course that St Michael's has just launched, and pray for that. Prayer is more interesting, and the congregations are becoming much more aware of each other.

Church leaders together

Behind the scenes, church leaders from across the city meet every month for prayer. Most churches are represented, though one or two stay aloof. Leaders respect each other's theological and denominational differences, and see their diversity as a strength. Each person brings to the table another angle on God's truth. They work together to think strategically about the city's needs, and how the church as a whole can respond to them.

They have a particular eye for unreached groups of people. 'What about the homeless people?' one leader asks. 'Is it really enough to do a nightly soup round? Shouldn't we be thinking about a night shelter, and eventually use that as a base for a new evening congregation?' The idea is prayed through, slowly takes root and then the different churches collaborate to bring it about.

A Salvation Army captain is the obvious person to lead it. No one minds that the project will end up under the Salvation Army wing. The other denominations have planted new congregations with backing from across the city. Everyone knows that if they work together opportunities will emerge for their denomination to sprout a new church. But if a church refuses to cooperate it will be left in the cold, without the resources of the other congregations to start something new. In any case, the late twentieth-century trend for people to be less denominationally minded has accelerated. Demarcation lines have continued to blur.

Forward to the past

'Nottingham in 2020' is certainly not nirvana. Older people complain about the age segmentation of church. They would love to worship with people of all ages. 'But would you be willing to worship in the music style and culture of a 20-year-old?' is thrown back at them when they complain. 'If so, you are welcome to join us! If not, and you want us to all worship together, are you assuming that it will be in *your* style? Why should you impose your style on us?'

Attempts are being made to bring the age groups together for events such as an all-age picnic (with a short communion at the beginning) and a day at a leisure centre. This is proving quite successful, but some older people still miss the children at church. Should the church be blamed for this segmentation, others ask, or does it reflect the nature of our fallen society? Others again wonder whether the church should be doing more – in a host of ways – to be counter-cultural. 'Are we really salt and light?'

Shades of the New Testament

Despite its limitations, there is much that echoes the New Testament church. Using networks to build congregations is reminiscent of how Paul launched his evangelism from the synagogue. He went to the Jews and to God-fearing Greeks who also worshipped there (e.g. Acts 17:1–4), making the most of his networks. He became a Jew to the Jews and a Gentile to the Gentiles, embracing cultural diversity for the sake of the gospel (1 Corinthians 9:19–23). No one-size-fits-all for Paul!

The congregations which mushroomed in his wake were based on networks which reflected the organisation of society. Christians met in people's homes, the basic unit of society (e.g. Romans 16:5). In Rome, where guild life was particularly strong and often concentrated in particular districts, two kinds of smaller Christian group may have existed – the work group and the house-church.[2]

These fragments of church were held together by occasional meetings together (1 Corinthians 14:23), by visits from members of different congregations (e.g. Romans 16:1–2), by letters from Paul and others, by providing mutual support like financial aid for the Jerusalem church, and by the oversight of the Apostles. Church was both fragmented and connected.

Shades of the it-must-fit-me world

The 2020 church also mirrors the two sides of personalised scale. Size and customisation come together. Cooperation between local churches enables church as a whole to harness the benefits of scale. Established congregations can pool their resources of prayer, money, gifts and time. These are then used to support fresh forms of church, built around particular groups of people.

Church is better placed to help people with their everyday choices – to become an 'agent'. That is because it is more focused on specific groups than traditional church: it is closer to people and is taking the trouble to research their needs. In particular, it is more sensitive to the differences between people in their work and their consumer settings, and has begun to develop distinctive approaches to each.

Standardised church is a glint in a rear-view mirror. Today we have an it-must-fit-me church for an individually wrapped world.

In your dreams?

Connected fragments were the essence of the New Testament church. They are typical too of 'Nottingham in 2020'. The latter is not perfect, but it has a heart for the socially excluded, it connects with different sections of society, there is unity in its diversity and – not least – Christianity has made a comeback.

Is it wishful thinking, or could this be a glimpse of the future?

Notes

1 Kees van der Heijden, *Scenarios: The Art of Strategic Conversation,* Wiley, 1996, pp. 199–202.
2 Robert Banks, *Paul's Idea of Community*, Paternoster, 1980, pp. 39–40.

CHAPTER EIGHT

FRAGMENTS OF TOMORROW

Dreaming is all very well, but was 'Nottingham in 2020' no more than that? The answer is that in Britain new forms of church are being trialled – not in large numbers, but enough perhaps to sketch the faint outline of a picture not so different from 'Nottingham in 2020'. Might church be on the edge of a dramatic new future?

The end of clones?

Church planting is one part of the picture. It involves reaching into new networks. Few people from a housing estate attend their local church for example, so a new congregation is formed among them. Or a new congregation is planted in a school to reach an unchurched network of families. Typical church plants are targeted at particular groups of people.

Our mould for you

In recent years all the major denominations in Britain have placed considerable emphasis on church planting. The Archbishop of Canterbury gave it his blessing at a conference in May 1991. The Elim Pentecostal Church has had a special focus on church planting, especially in north west England.

Kensington Temple has started many new churches in and around London. Various new church streams see church planting as a crucial method of evangelism.[1]

But many of these plants have failed to realise their potential, and the number of new plants has declined in recent years. Often plants have been replicas of existing congregations, or reactions against them.[2] Instead of moulding the plant around the people it was designed to attract, newcomers have been expected to fit into a model that suited the Christians setting it up. The core either copied what they already had or sought to create what was missing from their 'home' church.

The new congregation was not built *with*, let alone *by* the people it was seeking to reach: it was designed *for* them. And very often the design did not fit, so the expected newcomers failed to arrive. Plants were not sufficiently personalised to the target group.

We listened to the wrong people

In the early '90s, as a minister in Taunton, I made exactly that mistake when we established a new 'Family Praise' congregation. Most of the people behind it were long-standing Christians. They wanted more informal worship than was available in our other services, and a longer sermon.

One or two people had a more radical vision. They wanted to build a congregation round people who did not come regularly to church, but were on our fringe. The congregation would have been very informal indeed, the music would have been more low key and the 'sermon' (if that's what it was) would have been bite-sized and taken less for granted. The congregation would have developed flexibly, acquiring its own style as it found its feet.

This was certainly not what the established Christians wanted, and with my support they won the day. The new congregation attracted a few on the fringe, and even more regular worshippers from other churches, but it was not a great evangelistic success. We had first decided what we wanted, then invited others to join. Perhaps we would have done better to have thought more carefully about those on the fringe.

Are lessons being learnt?

Bite-sized churches

Spurgeon's College and Oasis Trust are placing teams of mainly young people in under-churched areas of East London. They live and work in the area, getting involved in youth clubs, football clubs and community activities. They worship in homes, but refuse to use the term church till it is given to them and owned by local people. One group didn't give themselves any name, but waited for people in the area to name them. The name their neighbours eventually settled on, Cable Street Community Church, came as a surprise. Here is one bottom-up approach to church planting which could be a model for the future.[3]

Teen churches

My church in Taunton must have been one of the first churches to establish a teenage congregation. Launched in 1991, we called it Nite Life. In its heyday it attracted up to 150 teenagers on a Sunday evening. On alternate Sundays the programme included a celebration, followed by a non-alcoholic bar, games and other activities. On the intervening Sundays the young people met in small groups, each led by one of their peers supported by an adult in the background.

It was incredibly hard work! There were all sorts of problems, and after several mistakes numbers dropped to 40 or less. So we decided to reinvent it. The young people gave Nite Life a new name, we involved them more closely in the design, we changed the venue, we worked more effectively with other churches, we staffed it more adequately and in 1996 we sprang it on the town as 'Uncaged'. Again it was a huge success for a while.

Peer pressure for church

Teenage and youth congregations of various kinds can now be spotted all over Britain. One estimate in 2000 put the total at around 100. They include the 'Soul Survivor' network of youth churches (headquarters in Watford) and Revelation Youth Church in Chichester. Growth from a handful to a hundred in a few years is not bad! The figure may be much higher. The 1998 English Church Attendance Survey (completed by a third of all churches) found that one in seven held a regular youth worship service, with an average attendance of 43.[4]

A great advantage of these congregations is that peer pressure can work in the church's favour. A fourteen-year-old looking round a traditional youth group of ten will not find it hard to conclude that he really is the exception. Scarcely anyone else from school is there. But attending a high-voltage youth congregation of a hundred plus is very different. 'This is a happening place!'

We can't expect teenagers to worship regularly with adults when they are separating from parents and reacting against adult life. Nor should we let them drift away from church because there is nothing for them. Is it not better to allow them to rebel against adult church by forming their own congregation in which their distinctive spiritual needs can be met?

Doing it together

But teenage congregations can be immensely difficult to sustain. They are inherently unstable – youngsters come and go and make all sorts of demands. They require close supervision, but of a kind that allow teenagers plenty of space. Adults need to understand youthwork, which these days means that at least one adult member per congregation will be professionally trained. For these and other reasons, teenage congregations usually require a number of churches to work together. Few churches have the resources to go it alone.

Teenage congregations can stem the flight of young people from church and attract youngsters who are totally unchurched. They could help revive the church if adults captured the vision, worked with other churches, made resources available and allowed teenagers to discover church for themselves.

Seeking or serving?

A very different beacon has been experiments with seeker services, inspired by the Willow Creek Community Church in Chicago. Willow Creek uses drama, music, audio-visual media, testimonies and 'issue-based' preaching to create presentations to audiences rather than participatory events. These services for 'unchurched people' are the main activities on Sunday, with worship and activities for nurturing faith occurring midweek. A number of churches in Australia, Britain and the United States are trying something similar.

At your service?

The Willow Creek mission statement, 'A church for the unchurched', expresses the priority given to non-members over members. The use of modern media in the presentations illustrates the commitment to cultural relevance. 'Process' rather than 'crisis' evangelism is highly prized: Willow Creek accept that people enter faith over time, offer an explicit welcome 'regardless of where people are at on their spiritual journey' and seek to work patiently with them. They have an 'Axis Service' tailored specifically to the needs of 'GenX'.

Willow Creek models the call to serve those on the outside patiently and with cultural sensitivity. By taking seriously the particular needs of specific groups – in particular Generation X – it connects with the 'it must fit me' expectations of our emerging culture.

Too sales savvy

However, one danger is that Willow Creek imitators will get locked into a 'we'll organise a presentation for you' mindset – believers 'market' the gospel to non-believers. This may become tough-going as people become increasingly suspicious of organisations that try to sell them things.

Winston Fletcher, a leading UK advertising executive, reckons that by the age of ten, children will have seen 50,000 different commercials about half-a-dozen times each. This is breeding adults who will be so distrustful of sales campaigns that they will flit from one brand to another. Marketers fear that customer loyalty is becoming a thing of the past.

Slick presentations of the gospel to unchurched audiences risk the response, 'You are just like any other organisation trying to sell me something.' Instead of generating 'customer loyalty' to Christ and his church, they may feed a consumerist pick-and-mix reaction. 'That was all very interesting. I liked what you said about relationships. I'll add that to my way of thinking' rather than, 'I feel grasped by something here. Do I need to change my way of thinking?'

Meeting people on their own turf

It is said that Willow Creek is most effective in reaching people who used to attend church or still come occasionally.[5] It seems to have less impact on those who have never been to church, a segment of advanced society that is growing rapidly. Is this because, despite its commitment to relational evangelism, it relies on a 'sales' approach that in the long-term is doomed to failure in our consumer-savvy world?

Marketers realise that if people are to trust an organisation they need to be convinced it is on their side. This applies as much to church as it does to Canada Life. Prepackaged presentations of the gospel won't cut much ice with people who are shaped by a culture that is profoundly suspicious. The new generations are wary of becoming committed lest they are betrayed, hurt or squeezed into a mould. They are most likely to be committed if they feel it is their church.

So how can the church persuade the unchurched that it is on their side? Encouraging non-believers to feel some kind of ownership of the church as they travel into faith is vital. Witness must be self-evidently altruistic. Christians must become not recruiters but friends – fellow-travellers, admitting that their knowledge is partial and their obedience inconsistent. Such frankness, says church growth professor Eddie Gibbs, will strengthen our testimony among those who look for honesty and authenticity.[6]

Willow Creek's commitment to cultural relevance has much to teach the wider church. But instead of being 'church *for* the unchurched', Willow Creek's imitators might do better to become 'church *of* the unchurched'. This would involve drawing closer to non-believers, sharing more of their lives and crucially, if they are willing to explore the Christian faith, giving them more freedom to develop expressions of the church that best suit them.

Willow Creek itself has an extensive programme among the poor. Why not encourage a group of poor people to form their own congregation rather than attend what may look like someone else's middle-class church? Perhaps people need to feel they belong to church before they are asked to join.

Belonging before joining

There is an element of being church before you have joined in Alpha, the ten-week introductory course to Christianity which involved over 6,300 UK churches in 1998–99. During an Alpha evening there is a presentation of the gospel, but the emphasis is on building community.

Groups that won't go away

The evening starts with a supper, next there is the presentation and then people break into small groups, supposedly to discuss the presentation. In practice, the groups have no fixed agenda. Members can talk about what they want, and if they would prefer to adjourn to the pub for instance they are free to do so. It is within these groups that often new friendships are formed, mutual support develops and people begin to have an experience of church, even though they may not describe themselves as Christians. Church is customised to the group.

Once the course is finished, however, people are encouraged to attend normal church on Sunday. Some make the transition, but quite a few don't. All round the UK – in Hampshire and Oxfordshire for instance – there are examples of Alpha groups continuing to meet for worship, prayer, teaching, fellowship and pastoral support, but not going to regular church. The rest of the church longs for them eventually 'to join us', but it may be that they won't make the leap. Will they peter out because they are not adequately resourced, or will they continue with an existence divorced from the wider church?

Alpha congregations?

One or two Alpha courses are beginning to emerge as new congregations in their own right.

Christ Church, Merthyr Tydfil, Wales is planning a church plant in 2001. They have been promised a minister to oversee it, and it will comprise almost entirely people who have completed an Alpha course. The congregation will meet either in a school or a pub, there will be no prayer book or formal liturgy, it will feel very different to normal church, but it will retain links with the sending congregation. Instead of expecting Alpha graduates to attend traditional church which feels strange and culturally alien, they will form their own congregation in a style that suits them.

In September 1998 Holy Trinity, Margate established a separate church for people in the Alpha culture. New people had been coming to Holy Trinity, quite a few through Alpha courses. There was tension between these newcomers who wanted a more relational church, and those who were rooted in traditional Anglicanism. As a solution the diocese invited the minister, the Rev'd Kerry Thorpe, to establish a separate church, in a nearby school, for Alpha graduates and others who preferred something less traditional. The new church focuses on small, midweek groups who also meet together on Sunday – a classic cell-church model.

Could these examples herald a trend? Why bust a gut trying to persuade ex-Alphas to join mainstream church which has little appeal? They are already coming to a group midweek, enthusing about it and beginning to make the Christian journey. So why not encourage some of the larger groups to continue meeting during the week and to experiment with what it would mean for them to be church? In due course members could be taught about Christian giving, and be invited to help pay for a minister either to lead their group or start a new one. A new congregation would be in the making.

It would take the bottom-up, community element of Alpha to its logical conclusion. And it might work not only for Alpha, but for the Emmaus course and others like it.

Church at work

Imagine a large Alpha course, perhaps in London, nearing its end. Instead of being invited to a follow-up Alpha and to Sunday church, participants might be asked, 'Many of us have been enjoying ourselves together and some of you have been journeying into faith. Would you like to experiment now with being church? We realise that many of you are turned off by traditional church, so why don't we continue to meet and pioneer

In some respects the subject of the first seminar was quite obvious.

together a form of church that works for you? Why don't you show us how to do church?'

Church will train you – and employers will pay!

'As part of this,' the invitation might continue, 'why don't you tell us what issues you face at work? We'll then use our networks to find expert Christians to provide training events for you and your friends. Whatever the topic – combatting stress, managing change, improving people-management skills, or getting up to speed with the latest health and safety regulations – we'll find a specialist to teach you best practice. Then at the end they'll offer an optional session on spiritual resources that can help you to practise what you've just learnt.

'Here is a way for you to take Christianity into the workplace. It will help you to discover how what you're learning here on Wednesday evening can make a difference to Thursday morning. It will be something you can offer to your friends, so that all of you are more effective at work. It will be an easy way of introducing your friends to church. And it will be free – because as a training course employers will pay!'

Weekday church, held near people's places of work and addressing issues of work, has huge potential. Everyone has colleagues at work, many of them are under tremendous pressure, and there is a growing market for training courses that go beyond functional skills to address values and emotional well-being. Employment-based networks would work to the church's advantage.

Ingredients for a new mix

Is this an unrealistic dream? The ingredients are coming into place. Workplace church is rising up the agenda. In the City of London quite a few Christians meet in groups during the week, and are beginning to ask whether they can be church in a fuller sense. Pressures of work, not least the number of hours involved, make it difficult for many of them to be involved with church back home.

The workplace is becoming all-embracing, taking over more of people's lives as employers provide fitness centres, creches and other facilities. Some Christians are asking, 'If the workplace is becoming so important, shouldn't the church be more involved?' Others are wondering if God's interest in work can be given a more concrete expression by letting church flower more fully at work. All this is moving slowly in the direction of workplace congregations.

In London's Docklands a group of Christians meet every Wednesday. For many of them this is not worship as well as on Sundays, but instead of Sundays. It seems effectively to be evolving into a workplace congregation.[7] *ASDA in Liverpool open half an hour later one morning a week so that their staff can attend communion first.*

More and more people are finding midweek worship – in a variety of settings – attractive. In England it has become a significant trend.[8] As the recognition grows that Sunday church does not suit all Alpha graduates, midweek churches, building on successful Alpha groups, could prove one solution. Perhaps initially they will be based on larger Alpha courses which have enough 'critical mass' to make a new congregation viable.

Dr Bill and Frances Munro run stress management courses for a variety of organisations, including Britain's Inland Revenue. At the beginning of each one they promise to introduce participants to techniques that will help them reduce stress. 'At the end of the day,' they continue, 'we're going to offer you a one hour optional session. You're free to leave before it starts, but if you remain we'll show you some spiritual resources that will help you to put into practice what we've taught earlier in the day.' They find that 60% to 70% of people stay behind for a simple introduction to Christianity.[9]

Pulling these elements together would create a highly effective model for workplace church. Congregations would meet during the week, be close to people's places of work and minister to the workplace through training courses, mentoring and by other means. Could this, too, be part of the future?

Are we moving to midweek?

'On a Council Estate in Dartford, Kent an Anglican vicar started a service on Wednesday mornings. Matins at 9.30am. Whoever would come? About 25 mums regularly attend, the time convenient as they can arrive after they've dropped their children at school. They do

not come to church on Sunday, because their husbands don't want
to be tied to looking after the children in their absence.

Such stories could be multiplied many times. The English Church
Attendance Survey asked respondents if they had a regular midweek
worship service. 42% replied YES ... In 1979, 37% of churches held
at least one midweek meeting ... However, these included any kind
of midweek meeting, such as house groups, prayer meetings, etc. as
well as worship services, whereas the ECAS question was specific.
Nevertheless some of the 37% would have included worship services,
though the percentage is unknown and would have been lower.

It means that over the two decades in between, the percentage of
churches holding midweek *worship* services has increased. Perhaps
by 2003 many more churches will be having midweek worship
services!'[10]

Reaching its cell buy date?[11]

Cell churches are attracting a lot of interest in Britain and other
parts of the world. It is a way of doing church that centres on
the small group. A local church will comprise a group of cells.
Each cell typically has eight to fifteen members, meets weekly
and provides what most traditional churches offer – welcome,
worship, word and witness. It includes ministry, teaching (cells
in a church often use the same material), Holy Communion,
Baptism and pastoral care.

Cells and celebrations

A celebration, drawing the cells together, meets regularly but
not necessarily every week. It is important but, unlike traditional church, is not the focus. Cells are the essence of church.
The emphasis is on relational evangelism. The priority for each
cell is to attract new members. When it has reached a certain
size, the cell divides. Multiply and grow is the aim.

This is not without its problems. A well-bonded cell may have
a life and culture that non-believers find difficult to break into.
Established members may be further along their faith journey

than enquirers, who feel out of their depth. Newcomers are expected to join what already exists, but often they don't fit so they do not stay the course. Church is not built round them.

Even so, cell churches have been effective in some places.[12] Cells provide community and friendship in the midst of a lonely society. The combination of small group and large celebration echoes the 'Nottingham in 2020' vision of fragments linked to a larger whole.

Cell churches certainly have a place in tomorrow's landscape, but will they be so preoccupied with their cell life that the celebration is as outward looking as they get? Will they be able to join hands with other churches?

Dismembered body or linked arms?

If tomorrow's church was purely customised, it would be a disaster. Fragments of church would be scattered all over the place, but nothing would draw them together. Each church would be a niche, catering for a particular group of people in its own way. Where would the whole body of Christ find expression? The body would be dismembered.

Prayer nets – the new fashion

One of the exciting movements in Britain today is the burst of network prayer around the country. Most large cities – and many towns – now have an integrated prayer net, drawing Christians together from across the denominations. Manchester's Prayer Network for example covers the whole city and has been meeting quarterly. So many churches have got involved that it has had to break into independent networks for each main borough. In Loughborough all the churches came together for a mission in 2000, with 40 community prayer cells organised ecumenically.

Christians from Brazil and Argentina get very excited when they see what is happening. Revival in their countries was preceded by a similar upsurge in prayer. Could God be using this prayer explosion to prepare the ground for a spiritual break-through in Britain? There is a mounting sense that this prayer phase needs to move into a harvest phase, but there is also some uncertainty as to what this might mean in practice.

The end of do-it-alone

There are other concerns. A number of the networks have a strong revivalist theology and a charismatic style that other churches find off-putting. There is a genuine desire by the prayer nets to draw in others, but often they lack the language and theological flexibility to make this possible. Justice is high on many of their agendas, and this may make it easier to enter into partnership with liberals and catholics. Would a more radical, twenty-first century approach to mission also help to build bridges?

Few churches have the resources to reach out to all the groups in their area. In our networked society, often people belong to networks that jump across geographical boundaries. If a church ploughs its own locality alone, it will keep unearthing parts of a network, but each part will be too small to support outreach designed specifically for it. Carve a network into geographical segments, and the pieces are too minute to be the focus of mission. But join the pieces up, and a mission tailored to the group may become possible. Churches have to work together.

Collaboration is taken for granted in the world at large. Will prayer networks make it easier within the church?

Tomorrow's church today?

A variety of developments, then, potentially challenge existing ways of being church. It is as if pieces of the jigsaw are lying on the table. They are all different. Church planting is learning how to be 'bottom-up'. Teenage and youth congregations come in all shapes and sizes. Willow Creek has modelled cultural relevance. Alpha congregations may be on the horizon. The ingredients exist for innovative forms of work-based church. Cell churches model fragments coming together and being resourced by the larger whole. The spread of prayer nets may be saying goodbye to 'I'll do it on my own'.

Fit these pieces together and a picture begins to emerge of church becoming more geared to the fragments of society, with hints of greater cooperation at the same time. Might this herald a new vision for church?

Notes

1 Peter Brierley, *The Tide is Running Out*, Christian Research, 2000, p. 14.
2 Stuart Murray, *Church Planting. Laying Foundations*, Paternoster, 1998, pp. 124–28.
3 Stuart Murray and Anne Wilkinson-Hayes, *Hope from the Margins*, Grove Books, 2000, p. 13. I am grateful to Stuart Murray for filling in some of the details.
4 Brierley, *op. cit.*, p. 162.
5 Murray, *op. cit.*, pp. 140–41.
6 Eddie Gibbs, *ChurchNext*, IVP 2000, p. 30.
7 This is an offshoot of St Anne's Lime House, which is in the process of buying a boat to put on Canary Wharf to house their activities.
8 Brierley, *op. cit.*, pp. 157–62.
9 Further details can be obtained from Dr Bill and Frances Munro, SALT, The Istana, Freezeland Lane, Bexhill-on-Sea, East Sussex, TN39 5JD, UK.
10 Peter Brierley, *The Tide is Running Out,* Christian Research, 2000, pp. 157, 161.
11 George Lings, *Encounters on the Edge*, No. 3, The Sheffield Centre, Church Army.
12 For a readable account of one cell church read Howard Astin, *Body and Cell*, Monarch, 1998.

CHAPTER NINE

CHURCH 'R' US

'Living Proof' exists on the outskirts of Cardiff, Wales. A house group started some traditional church-based youth work in 1984. It grew till they were running clubs six days a week for all age groups. Following a visit to New Jersey in 1993, they began imparting life skills to young people by teaching them to care for younger people. This was done in several local schools, and in summer play schemes were set up involving 1,500 children over five weeks. Their catch phrase became 'everybody is special'.

The children noticed staff meeting for prayer and asked to join them. Living Proof weeks were introduced to bring youngsters into the faith, but where could they go for discipleship? They did not fit into local churches. Soon there were too many to squeeze into a house and they started meeting in a community centre. It was never the leaders' intention, but they discovered they had a church. Now the leaders have been ordained, and Living Proof is recognised as an Anglican church plant with an inter-denominational congregation.[1]

Here were Christians going to young people, responding to them rather than imposing a package on them, and building a congregation around them. It has been hailed as an outstanding example of a different way of being church – another piece

of the jigsaw. Join the pieces together and a new way of thinking about church could be about to emerge. Are we seeing the
birth of a new paradigm that will reconnect church to the
world? And if so, what are its ingredients?

From 'You come to us' to 'We'll come to you'

Two people in their mid-twenties with very little church background were invited to one of the London Alpha courses. They
loved it, so they went to the follow-up course. After two weeks
they stormed out, never to return. One of their complaints was
that they had been told they should go to church on Sunday.
'Now we know that the church is just like any other organisation. You're not interested in us, you just want us to come to
your thing.'

'Come to us, we love you' will not work any more. It runs
against the deep suspicion that people have of organisations,
especially younger people. They do not trust organisations to
put their interests first. They have watched thousands of commercials, learnt to see through them and know that organisations' loyalty is not ultimately towards them. They do not
expect the church to be any different. They are consumer-wise.

To reach people in the twenty-first century, church will have
to go to them and prove that it is on their side.

They keep falling off!

Most churches pay lip-service to 'we'll come to you', but in
practice they have a stepping-stones approach to evangelism
which is very different. They have a Mums & Tods group for
example, in which most of the mothers are non-churchgoers. So
they ask, 'How can we get these mums to church?' Perhaps they
show a video about parenting, then organise an evening talk on
the subject, next invite the parents to an Alpha supper, hope
that some will come to the Alpha course and wait for them
finally to arrive in church.

But so few make the journey! Most slip off the stones before they have jumped across. So why not try a different approach? Why not go into the mums' group, get to know the mothers well, talk about the children, ask if any of them have prayed with their children and use that as a starting-point?

'Would you like to see some of the Lion books of prayers for children, or their Bible story books that you can read with your children?' This might be an entrée to talk about the mothers' experiences of prayer – maybe the difficulties they have praying, or any examples they have had of answers to prayer.

So we'll do it your way

You might ask the mothers if they would like some of the retired people in the church to look after their children for a period, while they have a time of quietness. During the silence you might play some appropriate music, and with the mothers' permission invite the Spirit of God to be present with them. You might teach them what to expect when the Spirit draws close, and invite them to share their experiences afterwards if they would like.

By varying the music, you might discover what seems to draw them into worship. Perhaps they spend more time listening to Christian songs than singing them, but that can still be worship.

You might ask if they would like a session on learning how to pray, and if they would like to keep a record of what they prayed for and whether there were any answers. Later you might ask if they would like to learn more about the Bible. In time you might ask them what form of study is most helpful to them – whether they prefer listening to a tape, or a short talk (if the leader feels up to it) or a discussion using the various group Bible study aids available. You will then have cracked how to do the sermon!

'Our church'

Perhaps in due course you might ask if any of them would like to be baptised, or to reaffirm their baptism vows if that's more appropriate. There is no reason why the service shouldn't take place when the mums regularly meet. A short communion service could be included from time to time. Before you know where you are, if you travel at the mothers' pace, a new congregation will have been formed.

I was talking about this on one occasion. Afterwards a woman said to me, 'We did something just like that with our young mothers' group. It met on a Thursday. We didn't realise what we had done till we heard some of the mums describing the meeting as "going to church".'

People-friendly church

Instead of doing it our way, when our way may be at an inconvenient time and feel strange and awkward, why not 'do it your way' and allow a pre-existing group to travel into faith at their own pace, and in the process form their own congregation in their own style? There can be no question of forcing a group down this path: each group must decide for itself whether this is a journey it wishes to make.

Though this approach won't always be appropriate, it might work not only for a young mums' group, but for an older person's luncheon group, an after-school teenager club, or for a group with a common interest (watching films perhaps, which could launch a discussion series on spirituality).

Potentially any group, whether it has links with church or not, can be invited to explore Christian spirituality, or Christian ethics, or lifestyle from a Christian standpoint or how Christians view 'big questions' like the purpose of life – and from that evolve into a congregation.

After I had spoken at a conference, an evangelist from a large Baptist church said to me, 'This is the third time I have heard you speak on this.' I immediately commiserated – three times hearing the same talk sounded like an ordeal. 'Oh no!' he continued, 'what you said about the failure of stepping-stones evangelism has changed my whole way of thinking. We're completely revamping our evangelistic strategy on the lines you've been talking about.'

Enough faith to become church?

How much faith does a group need before it can consider itself a congregation?

Matthew 28:16–20, which contains the Great Commission, describes how the disciples had gathered on a mountain in Galilee. Jesus appeared to them, the disciples responded by worshipping him, 'but some doubted.' 'Some' can also be translated 'they', which means that even though Jesus was standing in front of them, possibly *all* the disciples still had doubts, not just a few of them.

What makes the account so remarkable is Jesus' response. He does not despair of the disciples nor rebuke them; he draws near to them. His body language demonstrates that he still accepts them. Then he issues his famous command to go and make disciples of all nations. Jesus' reaction to doubt is to tell his disciples to found a church!

People who explore Christianity for the first time will have lots of questions and lots of doubts. In this they will have plenty in common with many well-established Christians who find themselves puzzling over difficult questions and asking sometimes, 'Can I still believe?' Doubt has been the experience of believers all through the ages. Many of the greatest saints had doubts.

If throughout history doubting Christians have belonged to church and the doubting disciples founded church, surely it is all right for people exploring the faith to consider themselves a congregation (if that is what they want), even though they remain full of doubt?

The essential criterion is not the amount of faith people have, but where they focus. On the mountainside the doubting disciples worshipped Jesus.

From 'church on Sundays' to 'church on weekdays'

'We'll come to you' means going to people wherever they are. Often this will involve church that is not on Sunday. For example . . .

At Todmorton in England's Pennine foothills, a family commun-
ion service is held on Monday afternoons. Children arrive from
school after 3.30 for a drink and biscuits before the 4pm service,
which lasts half an hour. 'It provides an opportunity for people
who really can't get to church on Sunday . . .' reports the Vicar,
Canon Peter Calvert. 'It is family oriented, and because it's
simple and accessible to children, it's also simple and accessible
to parents. It has brought people into the worshipping life of the
church who find Sunday services a bit awesome, a bit wordy and
a bit middle class. It's a real growth point.' It attracts 100 or more
children and adults compared to Sunday's attendance of around
150. [2]

Midweek church, here it comes!

Midweek church has become more common in Britain over the
past 20 years,[3] and is set to expand substantially throughout the
advanced world over the next 20. What will fuel this?

* *The spread of shift work* will make regular Sunday church
  impossible for more people. Shift work is nothing new, but as
  we head into the 'twenty-four-hour society' more people will
  be working at weekends. Leisure will boom on the back of
  greater prosperity, creating more Sunday jobs in retailing,
  entertainment and leisure generally. More cars on the road
  will produce a traffic crunch in areas of high congestion – on
  current trends, Britain's main artery, the M1, will resemble a
  car park in 40 years' time. People who can are likely to spread
  their work over the whole week to avoid commuting during
  peak traffic.
* *More parents will separate.* Although divorce trends have lev-
  elled out in some advanced countries, more cohabiting
  couples are having children, and separation rates for these
  couples are higher than for marrieds. The separation trend
  for all parents together, cohabitees and marrieds, is likely to

continue upwards. More parents will be juggling the custody of children at weekends, and finding church on Sunday morning highly inconvenient.

• *More people will be away at weekends.* Greater prosperity will continue to make people more mobile at weekends. The ageing population will see more people off to visit their grandchildren. Younger people will be visiting family and friends. Weekend holiday breaks will become more popular. Regular church life will become more difficult if it is Sunday based.

• *More people will chill out on Sundays.* A growing number of people are finding that they work flat-out during the week; they socialise for several evenings, including Saturdays, daytime on Saturdays is used for domestic chores and Sunday becomes the day of recovery because there are no obligations. The Silicon Valley has bred 'sleep camels' – people who store up sleep for the weekends. Sunday church jars with this way of life.

• *More children will have sports and other activities on Sunday morning,* already a growing trend.

For many people Sunday morning church will be a real barrier. The unchurched will not come to church unless it is more flexible as to when it meets. For many years some Catholic churches have held family eucharists on early Saturday evening. An Anglican church, Christ Church Winchester, has just launched an all-age service at 5pm on Saturdays for those who can't get to church on Sundays.[4] Other times will suit other groups of people.

Sunday church will certainly not disappear, and there will always be some Sunday morning services. But even on Sundays the times are likely to change. Some Australian churches have switched services from Sunday morning to early Sunday evening, when people have returned from the beach and other activities. Not infrequently, after the late afternoon service families go off to McDonalds together, which strengthens fellowship.

Church in the shopping mall

Midweek church is likely to involve new types of congregation. In Deptford, south-east London, a group – originally from the Ichthus Fellowship – run a children's church on Saturday morning with up to 80 children. The gathering is led by children and supported by adults with songs, games and Bible stories. The aim is to do church through a child's eyes, rather than ask children to fit round adult structures. The demands of time and energy on a relatively small group of adults has forced the congregation to meet less often, but it illustrates another way of doing church.[5]

For many families with young children, shopping on Saturday morning is a nightmare. So why not start a children's congregation involving games, drama, dance, music and Bible stories, with an invitation for parents to drop off their kids and shop in peace? Occasional events could be held for parents, to offer them a taste of church too. The Salvation Army is working with children in one British supermarket. Could local churches work together to do something similar elsewhere?

Church at work

Should midweek church include church in the workplace? Certainly work-based churches are nothing new. Chaplaincies in hospitals, universities and the military, for example, provide regular worship for people at work. Opportunities for workplace church could well grow.

Alpha courses, for example, have been held successfully in the Bank of England and in the head offices of some of the large corporations in London. Might it make sense to hold more such courses (and not just in London)? Some could be encouraged to evolve into 'cell' congregations, resourced by a person with oversight over a number of cells. These cells might meet together from time to time in a larger celebration. They would evolve into a cell church.

Christians in the London office of what used to be Price Waterhouse, an international consultancy firm, had an arrangement that whoever was in the country would meet at an agreed time each week in a particular place. This was a meeting mainly for fellowship. But if Christians in a number of offices in an area had a similar arrangement, might this involve enough people to become a regular congregation? Members might keep in touch between meetings by praying and doing Bible study on-line.

Those in 'secular' employment who have also been ordained might have a role in initiating and overseeing such congregations.

The Church of the Saviour, Washington DC

'Here nine separate congregations have developed, each with its own ethos. They ask three questions: What is the mission in this downtown area of the city? What kind of community is needed to sustain the mission? And what set of spiritual disciplines is required to sustain that community in that mission?

'They have developed congregations around a hospital for street people, a job centre, a housing association, a coffee shop and book centre, an inter-generational home caring for the elderly, to name but a few. It is possible for someone to come off the street, and to move through the ministries of the various communities: to go through detox, to find accommodation and a job and a whole new beginning in life and faith.

'What unites the congregations as one church is the teaching and discipleship programme that they all share in, run by the Servant Leadership School – another mission congregation. This again has a unique flavour, for they have devised a highly contextualised approach to reading Scripture and allowing the context to shape the theology . . .'[6]

The congregations meet at different times of the week. The Eighth Day Community meets on Sundays and is full of musicians. The Jubilee Church meets on Monday nights and is a wild mix of black and white, rich and poor, Jew and Gentile, young and old. The Potter's House Church meets on Wednesday evenings in a coffee house and is more contemplative. A short sermon is pondered around the coffee tables over a communion meal of cheese and fruit. Dunamis has an emphasis on those carrying political responsibility.[7]

This celebrated example might be a model for city centre churches to explore: but it could also suggest a way of being church in the workplace. Congregations might be formed around different occupations, different employers or different localities where people worked. Each might be highly contextualised in its approach, and be supported by a centre with teaching and other resources.

Work – a fringe benefit for church?

Church at work rather than on Sunday will not suit everyone of course. Couples who work in different areas might find themselves worshipping in different congregations. Parents with children might want to worship as a family (though if children's congregations begin to multiply, all-age worship might decline). Yet for single people, for couples where one partner was a churchgoer and even for some couples where both partners attend church, workplace congregations could meet a need – at least for a while: people could always move on to a different form of church as their circumstances change.

Churches at work may be key for advancing the kingdom of God. Most of the decisions that vitally affect people's lives are taken at work – by investors, marketers, TV producers, teachers, politicians, doctors and many others. Consumers' hopes, tastes and expectations are interpreted at work. How to respond to these – whether to meet them, change them, or

forget them – is decided at work. New ways of satisfying consumers are devised at work.

Power in modern society is exercised at work. If Christians
want to change society, the priority must be to change what
happens – at work.

Yet the church is not organised to confront this power.
Although some Christians meet together at work for prayer,
being church – worship, ministry, fellowship, endless activity
and the organisation itself – occurs largely outside the workplace. The focus of church is away from work. The enemy is
massed in the jungle, but church is fighting on the plains. How
can all the power that is concentrated at work be redeemed
unless work itself becomes the context for church?

From 'missionary congregations' to missionaries

'Missionary congregations' was used by Robert Warren, when
he was the Church of England's National Officer for
Evangelism, to describe congregations that had radically
reworked themselves to be mission-focused. The congregation
proclaimed the gospel as much by being church, in the quality
of its spirituality, as by 'doing' church through active evangelism.[8]

There is much in the idea that is helpful. Many churches have
grown, and continue to do so by developing a mission-focused
spirituality. Turning themselves into 'missionary congregations' will remain the best strategy in some cases. But many
churches have become too disconnected from society for this
approach to work.

Can they ever grow?

I think of one particular congregation. It had a lovely atmosphere, God was clearly present in its worship and visiting
preachers commented on this. Yet humanly speaking, if you
looked at its age structure and the difficulty it had attracting

new people, you would have to conclude that its lifespan was about 30 years. By then, on current trends, it will be a tiny rump.

So what might one do? A minister might battle away to modernise the service and introduce other changes that would make the congregation more appealing. But there would be lots of opposition, people would be upset, and to be effective the changes would have to be so large that the congregation would end up worshipping in a style completely alien to them. Members would be so miserable that no outsider would want to join!

Of course it wouldn't come to that. There would be all sorts of compromises, a few small changes would be introduced, a slight change in the balance of music or 'the Peace' in a different style perhaps, but the result would be hardly worth the candle. The changes would too small to make the congregation a magnet for unbelievers.

So why bother? Why do ministers and congregations consume precious energy and good will, changing from one prayer book service to another or introducing a few more contemporary songs, when hardly a single newcomer will be added to the church as a result?

Why not a missionary instead?

Would it not be better to praise God that he is blessing the congregation as it is? Members might be encouraged to continue worshipping in a style that fits them, to face the reality that on current trends they may not have a long-term future and to respond by supporting a half- or even a full-time missionary, who would plant a new congregation which would grow even if theirs declined?

People who didn't want to change would not have to. Yet church growth would be secured through missionaries who would do what missionaries have so often done – go to unreached people groups and plant churches among them. Mission agencies in Britain have recognised the need for this in the UK by appointing mission partners to that country. Church Mission Society has more mission partners in Britain than in any other nation.

If today's shrivelling church is to become a growing one, the advanced world needs many more missionaries – children's workers, youth workers, workers in urban priority areas, missionaries to the workplace, missionaries to football supporters and many others. Instead of burdening static churches with guilt and urging them to grow when that may not be realistic, why don't leaders excite them with a more practical vision – the opportunity to give financially to the planting of a new congregation?

That will not suit everyone. Some churches are struggling just to keep their financial heads above water, let alone pay for another congregation. Yet many Christians will rise to a financial challenge if they can see how the money is going to be spent, and if the initiative is close to home.

From 'We'll do it alone' to 'We'll do it together'

For ten years I used to run up to three 'Just Looking' groups per year, for people who wanted to explore the Christian faith. In each group there were some people who already came to church, and normally quite a few who did not but whom I had got to know through my pastoral contacts. We would start with perhaps 20 in the group and end up with around 10, who would continue as a house group.

Very few of those who did not go to church at the beginning started going to church by the end. However hard I tried, and despite introducing more modern services, I failed almost completely to persuade the non-churchgoers to come to church. Many of them loved the group. They would come regularly from meeting to meeting. But they would not come to church.

In my final year I asked myself, 'Why am I trying to get these guys to church? Why don't I turn Just Looking into a congregation? Why don't I ask them if they would like to explore what it means to be church? And why don't I teach them about Christian giving so that they can pay for a part-time minister to lead them? I could then go off and start another group.'

The reason I didn't was that I thought a congregation of about ten was too small to be viable. (Cell church advocates might disagree, but that is how it seemed to me when thinking about the people involved.) So what would I do now, four years later?

Finding partners

I would start differently. I would network among my fellow clergy to find others who shared a similar vision. I would then work with them to run one Alpha, Emmaus or equivalent course for the town each year. The aim would be to attract 100 people initially, end up with 50 people and encourage those 50 to become a congregation, paying a part-time minister to lead them. Because ideally different denominations would be involved, the congregation might be Anglican in year one, Baptist in year two, Independent in year three, Methodist in year four and so on!

Few churches are big enough to respond to all the mission opportunities in their area – opportunities among young people, single parents, older people, people with disabilities, unemployed people and many others. Many of these groups jump locality – there are a handful of teenage mums in one area and a handful in the neigbourhood next door.

It can make more sense for several churches to look at the needs of a town or a large suburb as a whole. It may be easier to cater for whole groups of people in the area than expect each church to respond to parts of a group. Work among teenagers is a good example. A teenage congregation is more likely to attract large numbers, which will give it an attractive 'buzz', if it is organised on a town-wide basis rather than if it is organised by one church alone.

It can work

Eternity in Bracknell, near London, is one such congregation. It aims to get away from youth services which are organised periodically for young people by adults. The aim is to build a community of 11- to 16-year-olds around regular worship in which the young people are fully involved. Around 60 young people belong to eight cell groups, which meet as a congregation on Friday night for teaching, worship and sometimes holy communion. Significantly, it is a joint venture by a number of churches in the town.[9]

Society is becoming too fragmented for local churches to respond on their own. In the emerging world, churches will need to collaborate if they are to respond effectively to the needs of the different fragments. The universal church needs to *be* the universal church, working as a unit.

Church out of the box

All this adds up to a new paradigm for church (though in terms of mission to unreached people, much of it is very old). It is a risky approach because groups might become valued only if they have the potential to evolve into a congregation. That would indeed be a travesty of the gospel.

After our love for God, we are called above everything to love people. We are to love them for their instrinsic worth, not because they have the potential to become Christians (or to become better Christians). Our love for individuals and groups will often mean that we remain committed to them, even though they make spiritual decisions with which we profoundly disagree. Church must continue to walk alongside, and value people who are on journeys that don't lead them to church.

The new paradigm represents a shift from standardised to customised church. The top-down approach, 'We have some nice ideas about church, come and join us', doesn't work any more. We need a bottom-up strategy instead: 'we'll come to you' rather than 'you come to us', midweek rather than Sunday church, missionaries rather than missionary congregations, 'we'll do it together' instead of 'we'll do it on our own'. An approach on these lines is likely to connect church with the emerging world.

It would be church that is geared to the different needs of different groups; it would be church that understands that collaboration is necessary to customise; it would be church that is no longer stuck in mass society but has embraced the age of personalised scale; it would be tailor-made church for a tailor-made world – church whose members could say 'Church 'R' us'.

But would it be church based on Scripture?

Notes

1 Stuart Murray and Anne Wilkinson-Hayes, *Hope from the Margins. New Ways of Being Church*, Grove Books, 2000, pp. 8–9.
2 *Church Times*, 17 December 1999, p. 6.
3 See 'Are we moving to midweek', in chapter 8.
4 *The Winchester Way*, October 2000.
5 Murray and Wilkinson-Hayes, *op. cit.*, p. 10.
6 *Ibid.*, p. 12.
7 http://members.home.net/dlature/itseminary/wischris/slssch3c.htm.
8 Robert Warren, *Building Missionary Congregations*, Board of Mission of the General Synod of the Church of England, 1995.
9 George Lings, 'Eternity – the beginning', *Encounters on the Edge*, 4, Church Army, 1999.

CHAPTER TEN

FALLING OFF THE BIBLICAL TRACK?

Some people will be appalled at this radical approach to evangelism. 'Aren't you making too many compromises? Isn't your approach being driven by society rather than Scripture? You are selling out to the world instead of challenging it.'

Clearly we have started with social trends, partly because they create the context for mission but also because God is active in society. The Holy Spirit is busy in people's lives long before some of them come to Christian faith. Old Testament 'wisdom literature' – Proverbs, Ecclesiastes and so on – assumes that 'secular' wisdom is part of God's purposes. A discerning response to the world will be a response to what God is already doing here. Might the 'wisdom' of personalised scale be calling the church to adopt a different approach to evangelism?

Rooted in Scripture

Scripture points in the same radical direction. 'We'll come to you' was the only possible evangelistic strategy for the Apostles because church didn't exist: they had to go to people and form church round them. When someone became a Christian they told their families and friends, and so inevitably new congregations were based on the networks of the day – people's homes. Whole households converted at the same time (e.g. Acts 16:33).

Male and female, young and old, slave and master and – sometimes – Jew and Gentile worshipped together not so much, it seems, because there was a deliberate attempt to bring different people together, but because they belonged to the same household or were friends of people who met in a particular home. They were part of the same network, a network in which people were treated unequally – hence the strictures in Galatians 3:28, 'There is neither Jew nor Greek, slave nor free, male nor female . . .' The gospel was to transform relationships within existing networks.

The result was that practices varied between churches. We get a glimpse of this in churches' leadership arrangements. Some were run by prophets and teachers (Acts 13:1), others by elders (Titus 1:5), others by overseers and deacons (1 Timothy 3:1*ff*) and others by non-descript 'leaders'[1] (Hebrews 13:7). Different networks did different things.

But alongside this diversity was a strong emphasis on unity. How could the oneness of Christ's body find expression amid so many fragments? The answer, it appears, was by writing to each other (the letters of Paul and others), praying for one another (Hebrews 13:18), visiting each other (Colossians 4:7–9), giving financial support to churches in need (2 Corinthians 8) and providing oversight for groups of local churches (Titus 1:5).

Meetings of congregations together, though they occurred (1 Corinthians 14:23), seem not to have been the prime vehicle of unity: these other links were more important. Communication was central. Churches that were embedded in networks were held together by networks.

It is more important than ever that we listen to this New Testament witness, because increasingly today's church is in a similar position to the church two thousand years ago. For most of the 'West', including many parts of the United States, church has lost its dominant place in society. It hangs precariously on the edge. Like the first Christians, our task is not to revive a churched world but to reach an unchurched one. The New Testament shows us how to do it.

So what should drive a bottom-up approach to evangelism? Certainly there are lessons from the emerging world, but more important are lessons from Scripture.

'Even so' . . .

The complaint may persist, 'you are advocating so much fragmentation! Won't this be deeply damaging? Look at Northern Ireland and South Africa for example! Hasn't the church there often mirrored divisions in the wider community, and even deepened them, rather than bringing reconciliation? Won't tailoring church to the different pieces of society simply reinforce our culture's fragmentation? Aren't you downplaying the New Testament emphasis on unity?'

So have we misunderstood the New Testament? Is a bottom-up approach to evangelism a sell-out to cultural separation? What other questions does it raise about the nature of church, and can these questions be answered?[2]

Unity based on diversity

Far from dividing church, taking 'we'll come to you' seriously is more likely to promote genuine unity – first because it reflects the Bible's affirmation of diversity. For example, after the Flood we are told that God makes a covenant with Noah in which he repeats the blessing of Genesis 1:28*ff*. 'Then God blessed Noah and his sons, saying to them, "Be fruitful and increase in number and fill the earth . . ."' (Genesis 9:1*ff*).

Genesis 10 describes the outworking of this blessing. Three times it repeats the phrase, 'These are the descendants of . . . in their lands, with their own language, by their families, in their nations' (verses 5, 20, 31). This clearly affirms the value of different cultures, each with its own language.

It sets the scene for the story of Babel in chapter 11. The

people seek to make a name for themselves and to avoid being dispersed by building a tower that reaches up to heaven (vs 4). They are punished for their spiritual arrogance by being scattered (vs 8). The means of this scattering is the cultural diversity described in chapter 10 – they cannot understand each other's languages (vs 7). Something intrinsically good, cultural diversity, produces the punishment. It is not cultural diversity that is wrong in chapter 11, but the division it gives rise to.

Pentecost seeks to reverse this division by drawing different nations into one church. Significantly, the confusion produced by different languages is not overcome by the disciples speaking in a further language which every nationality can understand: rather, each person in the crowd hears their own language. The unity of the church is based on the converts' oneness in Christ, not on smoothing over linguistic and cultural differences.

Reconciliation means respecting differences

Throughout history, Christians have recognised that there is no good reason to draw converts completely out of their culture: they are to follow Christ within their culture, transforming it. When this has been forgotten, when missionaries have sought to impose 'Western' practices on converts in traditional societies for instance, there has rightly been criticism.

While this seems obvious for missionary work abroad, the principle often gets forgotten in missionary work at home. Unity becomes confused with uniformity. 'We must all worship in a similar way to express our unity in Christ.' But there can be no real unity when you ask people to give up their cultures and be the same as everyone else. You are not reconciled with your sister when you ask her to be the same as you.

Genuine reconciliation demands respect for the differences between people. We need to acknowledge the different cultures that exist for example between eight- to eleven-year-olds, teenagers and adults. From time to time we may want to bring all the generations together, but it will not be true reconciliation unless the various age groups are also allowed – at other times – to express their distinct cultures in, perhaps, their own particular worship styles.

If we deny diversity we deny respect, and our reconciliation becomes a sham. Monochrome church becomes a substitute for unity.

Unity based on empowerment

Even worse, claims the Rev'd Bob Hopkins, a church planting expert in England, if we deny diversity we open the door to domination. Who takes control if you bring lots of different people together? It is almost always those who are better educated or more affluent. They dominate the proceedings and set the tone.

Hopkins cites the experience of a church in a poor area of north-west England. It was making great strides in attracting people from the immediate community. It became seen as a successful church, and so middle-class Christians from further afield began to attend. After a couple of years, the original, working-class members started to leave. 'It doesn't feel the same any more' they complained. Unintentionally, the new arrivals had changed the culture, made it a little more 'bookish' and the less educated no longer felt at home. Many churches could echo that experience.

In our fallen world, when you bring people from different cultures together you almost always create an opportunity for the better educated and more wealthy to stifle the others, often unwittingly. The less privileged will have fewer opportunities to develop their gifts. A recent study of urban regeneration projects concluded, 'If the community is seen as homogeneous then only the most powerful voices will tend to be heard.'[3]

Parkwood Community Church in Chicago attracts second generation Asian American Christians, mainly Chinese and Koreans.

Members are trying to build on the gospel dimensions of their culture by building an extended-family church which affirms the values of respect, hospitality and courtesy. To do this they have had to break away from domination by the elderly who, for example, discourage younger leaders. The age of members is predominantly under 45. Sadly, church seems to work best for Asian Americans – up to 97% of whom are unchurched – only if the young meet separately.[4]

Diversity in the body – different congregations for different groups of people – provides an opportunity to avoid domination and to empower the weak.

Unity based on collaboration

The idea that unity should be based on people meeting in the same place is plainly absurd. You can't physically get everyone under the same roof!

Churches have long recognised that culturally different congregations should be allowed to meet separately. Where I ministered in Taunton, I was told that in as late as the 1950s the upper middle class worshipped on Sunday morning and the lower classes in the evening. The only time they came together was at harvest supper, which apparently was a nightmare!

As we have seen, unity in the New Testament church – to the extent that it existed – was not based on all the Christians meeting together in one place every week, but on different churches communicating with each other and collaborating where necessary. They prayed for each other, they sent messages to one another and when the Jerusalem church was in trouble they provided financial support.

Networked church

Might joined-up church, based on communication and collaboration, become easier in future? Thanks to paper-thin TV screens hanging from the wall, it will not be long before one congregation can share in the worship of another. A video clip will show a church plant what its sending congregation is doing. The price of these screens will steadily fall, enabling a growing number of churches to feel closer in touch.

In the emerging network society, no one will belong to just one network – and that will apply to church. Already plenty of opportunities exist to pull Christians together, and in future there will be many more. All-age barbecues, possibly with a short communion service, and other social events may in some cases prove more effective in bringing the generations together than the traditional all-age service once a month.

'Schools of Christian Studies' have been tried in some areas, enabling members of different congregations to study the faith in more depth. As society becomes better educated, they may become more popular – especially among retired people with more time.

In our hurry, hurry world more people are going on retreats, often with Christians from different backgrounds who also want time out with God. Special interest groups, from the healing ministry to Christians in business, are springing up. Networks that we cannot imagine now are likely to criss-cross congregations in future.

Unity could have a promising future. Rather than a church of isolated fragments, the network society could spawn a net-worked church. As Christians from different backgrounds intermingle, church could help to counter the fragmentation of tomorrow's world.

Joined-up church may be easier than ever before

- *Post-denominational attitudes* are spreading, thanks largely to society's more laid-back approach to truth and suspicion of institutions. Younger generations especially are less interested in denominational niceties. They expect churches to work together.

- *Local churches are doing more together* with the spread of prayer nets in Britain, and a series of joint ventures ranging from Pentecost parties to town-wide missions. This is building trust and creating a fund of positive memories.
- *Mission imperatives* will force cooperation. Some churches will not be able to survive on their own. Others may recognise that they lack the resources to reach out alone. Enterprising clergy, frustrated by the lack of opportunities in their local churches, may welcome collaboration because it provides an outlet for their energies. Fears of 'sheep stealing' may decline as cooperation encourages ministers to think in broader terms – 'my church may be declining but I'm helping to create a new church somewhere else', or 'my church is the town's church.'
- *Women clergy* will continue to become more numerous. They may find cooperation easier than men who are often more competitive.
- *Technology* will aid cooperation. Everyone can be kept in touch via email. In the next 10 to 20 years large flat TV screens, hanging from the wall, will enable one congregation to see what is going on in another – and pray for it. Although e-church is unlikely to replace physical church for most people, Christian interest groups will mushroom on-line, drawing people together.
- *People will keep moving on* as they constantly push back the boundaries. Consumers in the 'experience economy' will quickly become bored, and as now crave new experiences. TV producers will be on the look-out for game-shows that are ever more daring and outrageous. People will tire of the old and seek what's new. However undesirable aspects of this are, it will affect the behaviour of Christians. They will not expect to be in one congregation for the bulk of their lives. If they don't change church because of a job or house move, they may well do so because they want a fresh spiritual challenge. Moving church could become a sign of spiritual maturity. Rather than being confined to one fragment of church, believers will constantly move across the fragments. Making newcomers feel at home will become even more important if we are to reduce the numbers who drop out of church when they move.
- *More time for networks*. Technology automates the routine aspects

of life, leaving more time for people to do what they want. Mod cons and pre-cooked food, for example, have reduced the time spent in the kitchen. The Japanese are developing electronic mice which will scurry across your carpets, hoovering up the dust while you do something else. Because we are social creatures, contrary to what some expect we are likely to fill the extra time by doing things with other people. Life will still feel frenetically busy, but we shall be busy with others (making the quality of these relationships an important issue). Churchgoers could have more time to network.

Joined-up church will be hard work!

But working together will not be easy. How will congregations who accept women in leadership relate to congregations who don't, both claiming to be biblical? How will Gay and Lesbian Church cease to find themselves isolated? To be 'one church' in our fragmented world will mean living with diversity and having generous hearts towards those with very different views.

It will not be simple – but then it never has been! The Corinthian Christians struggled, and they were not the only ones – either then or since. In our fallen world there will always be a danger that the fragments of church will go their separate ways.

In most cases the solution will not be to try and mix every-one up week by week, shoe-horning them into standardised church. The very forces that pull the fragments apart will discourage people from mixing together. Church won't be full of very different people, it will be empty!

Instead we should welcome diversity for the benefits it brings, and furiously promote communication and cooperation between churches. Rather than having unrealistic hopes about drawing people into one place, the answer to fragmentation is to start with sinful people as they are, and to become more creative in encouraging different groups to be aware of each other. Awareness can then grow into mutual support.

Once people have learnt to cooperate in the security of their groups, they may gain the confidence to meet regularly with folk who are very different. Collaboration between groups could be a step to mixing the groups up. But we shall never get that mixture unless we go step by step first.

The end of denominations?

To reach the fragments of society, local churches will need to cooperate. No one church has the resources to respond to all the people groups in its vicinity, whereas churches working together might be able to impact a number of such groups. Would this cooperation spell the end of denominations? Might local churches draw closer and closer together, perhaps eventually forming local federations that would replace denominations?

These fears are easily exaggerated. It is more likely that denominations would continue to play an important role, first by authorising and training leaders. In an increasingly suspicious age, people will want to be reassured that they can trust the leadership of a congregation before they join it. 'It's not a cult, is it?' The ordination or licensing of leaders by well-established denominations will demonstrate that the leaders are in good standing. 'They're Methodists? I've heard of them.'

A bridge between the local church and wider world

Secondly, denominations provide a bridge between the local church and the wider world, including the wider church. They do this by representing the denomination to other churches, to the worldwide church, to government and to society generally (through spokespeople in the media for example). They also harness the resources of the denomination to support the local church through training – for instance, conferences and publications.

Some fear that this bridging role might be undermined if local churches collaborated too closely in planting new congregations. Local cooperation might weaken loyalty to the denomination and divert resources from it. The local church would rather give to the joint venture in the town than to the denomination. New converts would not grow up in the denomination's tradition.

But from a denomination's standpoint, being involved in collaborative church plants would create an opportunity for its members to lead some of the new plants. Because of their denominational ties, these leaders would be likely to draw converts towards their particular affiliation. Someone thinking of being ordained for example, would be encouraged to train within the leader's denomination. The congregation would provide financial support for the denomination, perhaps to pay for its leader's salary.

Collaboration would provide the opportunity for a denomination to share in church growth instead of being isolated and, as often now, experiencing decline.

A sense of identity?

Thirdly, denominations have traditionally impacted the local church by providing a sense of identity. Each denomination provides an ethos, a set of traditions which shapes the local church. A Catholic church will feel very different to a Vineyard one. This too would be likely to remain the case. Leaders working in collaborative church plants would be bound to bring their denominational backgrounds with them, which would influence the life of the plant. A Baptist minister would be unlikely to practise infant baptism!

In the cause of mission however denominations may have to become more relaxed about the amount of diversity they accept. In a fragmented world, how uniform can worship and other practices be? The Church of England has moved from a single set of services in the *Book of Common Prayer*, to greater diversity in the

Alternative Service Book to considerably more diversity in its new *Common Worship*. Many believe that the latter still does not go far enough, and that even more diversity will be necessary. In the it-must-fit-me world, new converts will not be drawn to an off-the-peg style of worship that fails to suit them.

Many denominations are wrestling with the threat diversity poses to their sense of identity. If member churches become increasingly different, what will be the thread that holds them together? An organisational structure? A basis of faith? Historic ties? Leaders networked together? Answers are likely to vary. What is clear is that if denominations are to encourage mission, they will need to free up the local church to respond to different people in different ways. Can we have denominations without domination?

Neighbourhood or network?

Does made-to-measure church mean that neighbourhood church is dead, to be replaced by congregations targeted at networks rather than places?

A world of differences

It is often said that with globalisation people do not belong to local communities any more; they belong to networks – and that the days of the neighbourhood church are numbered. But these claims are exaggerated.

Local communities are still important to people, and they will become even more so as globalisation strengthens people's attachment to the local. You may not know many people nearby as you surf the Net, commute to work and travel to meet friends. But faced with the complexities of 'McWorld', familiar landmarks near home – a take-away, the local radio station or a crossroads – will help you to identify with your particular part of the globe.

Landmarks are becoming so important that sociologists

Figure 4
People have little in common with their neighbours

'In general, how much would you say you have in common with the following?' (where 4 = a lot, 3 = a fair amount, 2 = only a little, 1 = virtually nothing)

People who have the same hobbies as you	2.82
Your parents	2.74
Your siblings	2.69
People who work at the same place as you	2.49
People who do the same type of job as you	2.44
People who enjoy the same type of television programmes as you	2.38
People who go to the same pubs as you	2.36
People who like the same music as you	2.31
People who are the same age as you	2.29
People with the same educational qualifications as you	2.17
People who read the same newspaper as you	2.07
People who support the same political party as you	1.97
People who wear the same kind of clothes as you	1.89
People who come from the same town or areas as you	**1.82**
Your neighbours	**1.81**

Source: *Planning for Social Change*, The Henley centre, 1995/96

speak of symbolic communities – communities which define themselves by their symbols. There could be an encouraging future for churches which attract people by providing a symbol of local belonging.

But it is also true that more people are joining dispersed networks, and these often loom larger in their lives than local communities (See Figure 4.). If church is to cater for everyone, we need congregations that are planted within these networks. Church would still be local, in its closeness to people, but not in a geographical sense. The Greek word from which we derive 'parochial' literally means 'someone who dwells alongside'. To dwell alongside people today includes plugging into their networks.

Room for both

To pitch neighbourhood against network ignores how nearly all the denominations embrace elements of both. The Church of England, based strongly on small geographical units, the parish, also has chaplains to networks in industry and in other occupations. Its mission to seamen will form a congregation on a particular ship at a particular time.

Free churches on the other hand seem to be more network-focused. But even they allow a role for geography when they avoid planting churches too close to one another in the same denomination. Some people will go to the current church because they live near it: better that the new one serve people further away.

In practice most denominations have been fairly pragmatic. When people's networks were geographically-based, churches tended to be established on a geographical basis, but where geography was less important other considerations have come into play. For the sake of mission this pragmatism should be welcomed. Where neighbourhoods remain important, let there be neighbourhood congregations. Where networks have assumed greater significance, let congregations be network-based.

When ministers are installed in the Church of England, the Bishop entrusts them with 'the care of souls'. Whether souls are cared for on a geographical basis or through networks, the key challenge is to make sure that everyone can be reached.

Church it ain't?

We have talked about letting groups evolve into a congregation, and have used the terms 'congregation' and 'church' almost interchangeably. But when does a group become a congregation, and a congregation become a church?

It is an important question because the labels we use affect people's attitudes. If we describe 30 young mums worshipping together on a Tuesday morning as a group, that will give them less status than a congregation. Church leaders tend to take more notice of congregations – and are more committed to being with them week by week: congregations have a more established feel to them than groups. Yet why should a congregation of thirteen worshipping first thing on a Sunday morning be regarded as more important than 30 mothers worshipping at a different time?

Perhaps more important, the mothers might get the message that what they are doing is not 'proper' church. It does not even deserve to be called a congregation. This will affect their expectations of what church can be. They will associate church with 'boring' worship on Sundays rather than with the more enjoyable things they do in their group.

We shoot ourselves in the foot when we use labels carelessly. If a group is acquiring church characteristics we need to give it a church-like label. Otherwise we make the statement, 'Church is something different', and people get the impression that church is not for them.

Therefore, for those pioneering new forms of church, how they describe their experiments will be one of the most strategic decisions they take. So what is the difference between a group, a congregation and a church?

Groups, congregations and churches

One might say that a group is any gathering that does not have the characteristics of a congregation! So what is a congregation? Perhaps we could say that a congregation is any gathering which has as its central activity the worship of the Trinitarian God. Other things will also be important – mission and fellowship for example – but worship will be at the heart of the congregation's life.

Different traditions will have their own slant on what

Christian worship should involve, but nearly all would agree that it should include praise, confession, prayer, ministry of the word, and the sacraments of baptism and holy communion.[5] These elements do not need to feature in every service, but they need to be present regularly.

A local church will comprise one or several congregations, and so inevitably it will have all the characteristics of a congregation. But in addition, it will have ties to the wider church. It is through the local church that a congregation becomes linked to the universal church.

The local church will usually be linked to a denomination or to a federation of churches. Frequently it will have links with other churches in its area and further afield. Its minister will be recognised by the wider church, normally through ordination or its equivalent. Congregations share in these wider links by being part of a local church, or in the case of single-congregation churches by simply being the local church.

Imagine that an evangelist gathers a group of enquirers. The group might eventually decide to become a worshipping congregation. As the congregation discovered how it was connected to the wider church (which might be paying the evangelist's salary for example) and could contribute to it, it would become aware of itself as part of the universal church, a local expression of church. If it was an independent gathering, it would see itself not as a group, nor as a congregation but as a church.

Church on a wide screen

So if what makes a congregation distinct is worship, perhaps what distinguishes a local church from a congregation is its connection to the wider church. The congregation is tied to the universal church by being part of a local church. In our fragmented society, this puts a helpful emphasis on the whole body of Christ. To be fully church, the local church needs to see itself as part of the universal church. This will encourage it to collaborate with other local churches and contribute to the mission of the church as a whole. It is not independent, but interdependent.

Drawing fragments together

The 'we'll come to you' paradigm of mission asks radical questions of church. What is the basis of unity between Christians? How should church be organised?

The paradigm promotes the oneness of the body because it demands unity with diversity, not uniformity. It seeks to empower the weak, not disempower them. It calls for unity to be based on collaboration, not concentrating different people in one place: networks should glue the fragments of church together.

It addresses questions of church organisation by affirming denominations, but resisting the domination of local church by them; by embracing both neighbourhood and network churches, not choosing between them; and by enabling 'congregation' and 'church' to become empowering labels that emphasise interdependence, not independence.

Church can join up the fragments of society – if it has joined the fragments of society first.

Notes

1 Stuart Murray, *Church Planting. Laying Foundations*, Paternoster, 1998, p. 83.
2 For a more general theology of church planting, see George Lings, *New Ground in Church Planting*, Grove Books, 1994 and Stuart Murray, *op. cit.*, pp. 27–61.
3 'Community participants' perspectives on involvement in area regeneration programmes', *Findings*, JRF, July 2000.
4 Further information can be found in Jeanette Yep *et al*, *Following Jesus Without Dishonouring Your Parents*, IVP,

1998, pp. 154–5. I am grateful to the Rev'd Jenny Petersen for this account of the church.

5 The Salvation Army and the Society of Friends have no sacraments and so they at least would want to nuance this definition.

CHAPTER ELEVEN

IMPLANTING A RADICAL GENETIC CODE

'I would like to be convinced' said the church leader, 'but I'm not sure that it would work. Despite all you have said about joining up the fragments, I can't help thinking that in practice the fragments of church would rip apart. By making so many concessions to the it-must-fit-me world, I wonder if we would ever persuade people not to be individualistic. Wouldn't we reinforce individualism instead?'

Others have expressed similar concerns. If we build church around tailor-made attitudes, won't we have sold the pass before we've begun? New congregations will be full of people expecting life to fit them perfectly. They will have little contact with established Christians whose values would challenge them. New congregations would be left to develop in their own way.

Might not the tailor-made mindset of new converts, far from being transformed by the gospel, subvert it instead? Converts would develop a form of Christianity that suited them exactly rather than allowing the Spirit to change them. Instead of discovering how they can fit God, new believers would make God fit them.

That at least is the fear – and it is not unrealistic. It takes seriously the grip of modern culture on people's lives. And it faces the challenge of history: many congregations have relished their freedom, only to go astray. How can we preserve doctrinal orthodoxy if tailor-made congregations evolve down their own path?

The big risk

What can be said in reply? Firstly, the fear seems to imply that the traffic is all one way – that new believers have lots to learn from the old-stagers. But don't established Christians have something to learn too from the questions, enthusiasm and fresh insights of enquirers? If we are going to object to new forms of church, let's at least do so on less patronising terms!

Crucially, the objection underestimates the power of the Holy Spirit to change people. History is full of examples of lives being transformed by God. One of my favourites used to be portrayed on a postcard in Fiji. It showed the great-great-grandchild of the last European to be eaten in the islands kneeling at the feet of the great-great-grandchild of the chief who had eaten him! It was thanks largely to Christianity that cannibalism was brought to an end in the Pacific – hardly an insignificant change.

When St Paul planted new churches, he taught them for a relatively short period, provided them with oversight and then left them to their own devices – and the devices of the Holy Spirit. In Corinth and elsewhere the new Christians quickly made mistakes, but Paul continued to trust the Spirit and honour the God-given freedom of the congregations. He seems to have understood that, like adolescents, Christians become mature by using their freedom and learning from their mistakes. His willingness to take risks challenges those who prefer to play for safety and control what's new.

There will always be disappointments, but we can expect that many who journey into faith will continue to have their lives changed, just as lives were turned inside out on the first Pentecost and have been so on countless occasions since.

Fostering cooperation

Steps can be taken to encourage faith-explorers to adopt biblical values, even before they have 'made a commitment'. This is particularly true of attitudes to cooperation.

Learning from the East End

Andrew Mawson is a doyen of Britain's 'social entrepreneurs', people with a gift for sparking community development. He is a United Reformed minister in Tower Hamlets, East London. When he started his ministry there were only a handful in the congregation. So he got their permission 'to try anything', and began catalysing one community initiative after another.

In a remarkable story, the number of community groups meeting on church premises grew from one to almost a hundred. The place is now a hive of activity throughout the week. They have built studios and workshops for groups of painters, sculptors, screen-printers, creators of stained glass windows and many others. One of Britain's poorest areas has given birth to one of the country's largest artistic communities – and in an area with over 40 different language groups!

While Andrew was telling me the story, he commented, 'We are committed to building community here. That means that when any group asks to use our buildings, we say to them, "You are very welcome, provided that each year you join with at least one other group on the premises to do something for the local community." That way' Andrew explained, 'we avoid having lots of isolated groups sharing the building. We start creating real community.'

Cooperation from the beginning

So here might be one possibility. Perhaps a church member draws together for evangelistic purposes a group of younger or older people, or a group with a particular interest. Once the group has formed, it might be suggested that from time to time they collaborate with another group to do something to benefit other people. Possibilities could range from carol singing to a fund-raising event.

That would enable the group, from an early stage, to develop the habit of cooperation and to show commitment to people outside. It would counter the fragmentation and selfishness of contemporary society.

What other Christian values could be built into a group? In the 'Just Looking' enquiry groups I led, after a few sessions I used to ask people to let someone in the group know if they could not attend a particular evening. That would not only be a common courtesy, I explained, it would show the others that they were not being taken for granted. If a crisis had blown up, it might provide an opportunity for the group to offer practical support. It would help us to be committed to one another.

Different values will be appropriate to different groups and will vary according to how long the group has met. But being explicit about the group's values, and negotiating them with other members, provides the chance to evolve a Christian ethos from the very beginning.

Creating the right expectations

How people are brought into the faith has a lasting impact on their spiritual journeys – 'we reproduce after our own kind'. If enquirers are told that Christianity is mainly about a personal relationship with Christ, that will shape their approach for years. They will tend to develop an individualistic faith. If, from a different tradition, they are told that Christianity is mainly about encountering Christ through the sacraments, their faith will have a stronger church focus. If, from yet another tradition, they are told that Christianity is primarily about social action, issues of justice will dominate their Christian lives.

Of course all three dimensions are vital. Yet as enquirers

explore the faith, what emphasis is given to each will profoundly affect whether new converts ape the individualism of today's world – or challenge it.

The process of conversion

I was brought up in an evangelical tradition where it was assumed that the process of conversion went something like this: first you converted to Christ, then to his church and then to his cause. Evangelists emphasised a personal relationship with Jesus.

This made sense when churches seemed to contain people who attended periodically on Sundays, embraced Christian values but had not encountered God in a personal way. Much evangelism was directed at those who had some contact with church. It tried to persuade them to move on – in the cliché of the day – from 'churchianity' to Christianity.

The situation today is different. Evangelism is increasingly directed towards people with very little church background. They live in a highly individualistic culture that majors on personal experience. So conversion involving a personal experience of God poses no problem – that's the easy bit. The rub comes when they are asked to surrender some of their individualism, place themselves under an outside authority and focus more strongly on self-sacrifice. Converting to the church and to Christ's cause is quite a challenge.

Faith-explorers will be helped to meet the challenge if they have positive experiences of 'church'. If they feel comfortable in the group, enjoy other members' company and trust them, they will be more willing to embrace the norms of the group and sign up to its 'cause'. The group will become a context in which they can discover how to experience God, develop a relationship with him and learn how to follow him.

Perhaps the sequence should be not to convert to Christ and then to his church, but to 'convert' first to church – and then to Christ and his cause.

Experiencing church

That is something of the picture we get in the New Testament. During Christ's ministry, it is hard to imagine any of his followers having a personal relationship with him on their own. They related to him in the context of a group, by joining the band of disciples that travelled with him.

We read of the group narrowing down to three people on occasions – Peter, James and John – but there are very few times when Jesus has a one-to-one with someone away from the group. When he does, as with Peter at the end of John's Gospel, the individual is drawn out of the group, but only for a while. The group remains the prime context for relating to Christ.

That is typically the case for new Christians today. Sometimes a person with no church connection will encounter Christ entirely on their own, but that is highly unusual. Most people do so in the context of church. They have been going to church for some time, and then find themselves drawn to Jesus and what he stands for.

This is what happens on Alpha, and on other courses like it, such as the Emmaus course. People taste something of church life – the fellowship, some learning and the beginnings of worship, and this makes them open to experience Jesus personally. Implicitly they convert to church before they convert to Christ.

Explain what's happening!

Explaining this process to enquirers may help them to form realistic expectations. What sometimes happens is that the initial teaching focuses on the individual's relationship with Christ, and the group dimension of faith is not made explicit. Faith-explorers end up with a confused message.

They enjoy the group, but what they hear is that Christianity is not mostly about groups, it is about personal experiences.

This reinforces their individualistic outlook and creates unhealthy expectations of what Christianity is about. By the time the teaching about church comes along, people have got it firmly in their minds that church is of secondary importance to the individual's experience – 'If it is so important, why hasn't it been made more of earlier?'

This makes it harder for new converts to attach a high priority to church – for example, taking on board what the body of Christians believe rather than developing their own individualistic versions of the faith, working through difficult relationships in church rather than allowing them to fester, remaining loyal to the congregation through difficult times rather than church-hopping to somewhere more exciting, and assuming the obligations of church membership rather than just seeking to maximise its benefits.

Expectations might be different if, from the earliest days, enquirers' experience of the group was matched by teaching about its importance. 'We want you to really enjoy the group because group life is at the heart of Christianity' members might be told. 'Being with others is the context in which we can discover how to have a personal relationship with Christ, and how our lives can contribute to his plans for improving the world. So in our sessions together, I hope we'll learn from each other how to have a good time – many of you, I'm sure, will have suggestions on how we can enrich the quality of our time together . . .'

Embracing the whole

Regular reminders about the importance of church, suggestions perhaps that the group is beginning to model itself upon a church ('which will help you decide if it's the sort of thing you want to join') and periodic discussions about the values that should inform the group's life will help to counter the individualism of members.

The group will be initiated into a Trinitarian faith where

equal weight is given to the Kingdom of God, the body of Christ and experience through the Spirit.

Challenging the it-must-fit-me world

In his classic book, *The Logic of Evangelism,* American theologian William Abraham shows that evangelism is not mainly about proclamation, nor is it primarily about church growth: it is about initiating people into the Kingdom of God. Evangelism is a process of instruction, of incorporation into the church and of participation in the works of the Spirit. It equips individuals to stand against the ravages of modern society and to advance the Kingdom.[1]

If new believers are to do this, they will need to be discerning about the cultures in which they live. They will need the support, encouragement and instruction of a Christian community as they learn to distinguish between healthy and unhealthy aspects of society, and develop a distinctive lifestyle in response. They will need to strike a balance, as Jesus did, between loving the world and challenging it. This will require them to critique the emerging world of personalised scale.[2]

Thinking about justice

There will be elements of this world that Christians can affirm. Organisations are beginning to relate to people in new ways, and that includes listening to individuals and taking them more seriously. Mass society said, 'You come to us on our terms. We have something to offer you. It may not be exactly what you want, so we'll use advertising and other techniques to persuade [manipulate?] you to take it.'

Under personalised scale, organisations seek to tailor their offerings more closely to what people want. Either they claim, 'We have listened to you and researched your exact requirements' or they say, 'We recognise that you know best, so we'll provide alternatives and let *you* choose'.

On the other hand, the deacons argued, why change a winning formula?

As this approach spreads, will it influence conceptions of justice? One criticism that can be made of the fashionable term 'social exclusion', which refers to people on the edge of society, is that it can imply a 'you come to us' approach. Combatting social exclusion becomes a way of saying, 'We'll find ways of drawing you into *our* society on our terms' – an attitude that belongs to the standardised world ('We'll treat everyone the same').

A tailor-made approach might say 'We'll listen to you and provide what *you* want. If you prefer to be different and not join our society on our terms, then we'll celebrate our diversity and learn somehow to live together.' This is a much more permissive view of justice than the one many are used to. Working through its implications presents huge difficulties, but at least it starts at the right point: it listens to those on the edge. In that it resonates with the gospel. How many times did Jesus ask people if they wanted to be healed?

Thinking about fulfilment

Jesus promised fullness of life, and this must include the opportunity for people to fully express God's image in them. The it-must-fit-me world will expand the possibilities for doing this.

Instead of being forced into a mould, individuals will have more chance to relate to organisations in ways that fit them. This will offer them new opportunities to express themselves – whether it is wearing T-shirts sporting their own choice of photos, or taking greater control over their work, or studying in their own preferred learning style. Though some examples may seem trivial, the whole adds up to a more expressive life.

In the 1960s 'pseud' was a term of abuse in Britain. It meant that you were not being yourself – yourself as defined by your background. You were getting 'above yourself'. Today people increasingly define themselves by being different to their backgrounds – and that will be true of more people in future. They will have more control over who they are – a dimension of the Genesis 1:28 mandate giving people dominion over the world. How can you have dominion over the world if you don't have dominion over yourself?

God's image is particularly expressed through relationships. It is given to the man and the woman together (Genesis 1:27) They reflect God as they relate to one another. New technology, an essential part of the tailor-made world, will provide more time for relationships. Research shows that people are spending longer with each other at work, as routine tasks are automated and more complex ones are accomplished by teams.

Likewise, technology speeds up routine tasks at home, creating more space to do what you want. Because most people enjoy being with others, this extra time will be spent doing

things in other people's company. Electronic games manufacturers, for example, expect these games to be played increasingly with other people rather than on one's own. Life will
continue to feel frantically busy, but it will be busy-ness with
people.

The quality of these relationships will be a vital question, but
the fact that we shall have more time for them is a welcome
trend. It will provide new openings to reflect God's image.

Thinking about individuality

The German theologian, Jürgen Moltmann, reminds us that we
first encounter the Trinity – either in our experience or in
Scripture – as three persons. The Son reveals the Father, the
Spirit fills believers. Each person is distinct.

Yet what makes their distinctiveness possible is the unity
between them – a unity that is based on their relationships.
Jesus could not be the Son if he did not have a Father, and of
course the Father would not be the Father without a Son. The
Spirit would not be active in our lives if he had not been sent.
The distinctiveness of each member of the Trinity is made possible by their relationships in the larger whole.

This finds some echoes in personalised scale, where larger
units also enhance individuality. One example is the sheer
number of people using the Internet. This enables someone
with a niche interest to find others who share that interest, to
develop it with them and to enhance a distinctive feature of
their personality as a result.

Cooperation between church leaders in a town might enable
one of them, with a gift of working among deaf people for
example to develop a particular ministry towards the deaf on a
town-wide basis. The distinctive ministry of that leader would
be made possible by relationships in the larger whole.

In particular, the Trinity relates to us in ways that enhance
our individuality. The Spirit releases gifts within the individual,
for instance. As organisations relate to people on a more

personalised basis, individuals will have more opportunity to express their distinctiveness. It will be a further way in which the emerging world will reflect the Godhead and its values.

Thinking about justice – again

But other dimensions of this world will be deeply hostile to the gospel. Justice is at the heart of God's character, but it is far from being at the heart of personalised scale. The priority for the tailor-made society will be to fit a person exactly: consumers will demand to be satisfied. Organisations will be preoccupied with meeting these expectations. Issues of justice will slide further down the cultural agenda.

In mass society, standardised approaches encouraged the expectation that people should be treated the same. Healthcare (if publicly provided), welfare benefits and taxes should be roughly the same around the country or state. This created a mindset that was more open to pleas for social equality. Sameness and equality came from a common stable.

In the tailor-made world, however, it-must-fit-me-exactly expectations will make diversity more acceptable. Giving people just what they want will seem more important than promoting equality. As rising inequality becomes accepted, concepts of justice may be redefined – 'there is nothing wrong with poverty in itself, as long as the poor have the absolute necessities of life'.

In Europe and Australasia especially, traditional Christian approaches to justice have tended to stress equality. These approaches could be marginalised under the influence of personalised scale. How should Christians respond?

Debasing relationships

Although more time is becoming available for relationships, tailor-made values threaten their quality. It-must-fit-me-exactly attitudes sit uneasily with Christian concepts of service. They will encourage 'me first' expectations which will make it harder to empathise with other people, put them first and trust them.

They will make relationships more transient. The post-1960s rise in divorce owes much to higher expectations of marriage. 'It must fit me exactly' will add to the strain. 'Our relationship isn't quite what it used to be; perhaps we should go our separate ways.' The same outlook will weaken commitment to social groups and networks. 'This group no longer meets my needs; it's time to move on.' Loyalty will seem distinctly old-fashioned.

In the attempt to personalise their products, companies are likely to debase the language of relationships. There are signs of this already. Management-speak refers to 'relationship marketing', but this is seldom a relationship based on mutuality and genuine care for the individual. The customer is valued only so long as they buy the product.

Organisations present themselves as friendly, but often this is pseudo-friendship. 'Dream hotels offer Michael Moynagh a cordial welcome' announces the bedroom TV. But the idea that the hotel is really interested in me is all-too-often belied by the service, while no one for a moment would imagine that the hotel is interested in them as a person.

As relational language is pressed into the service of economics, cynicism will mount. Customer loyalty will be harder to maintain. Businesses will have to spend ever increasing amounts on retaining customers, or winning new ones to replace those they have lost. Will more firms struggle to keep enough customers to stay in business, and will this make the system more unstable?

Customising God

The made-to-measure mindset may also encourage a customised view of God. People will be more likely to look for a God that suits them exactly, a God who is created in their image and not his. This will open the door to new forms of idolatry. Discipleship may become more difficult as people shy away from uncomfortable aspects of God's character.

So some aspects of the emerging world will resonate with the gospel – organisations listening more carefully to people, giving them more opportunities to express themselves and echoing the Trinity in the use of scale to enhance individuality. But other aspects will collide with the gospel – less concern with justice and equality, less commitment within relationships and more cynicism, and a stronger desire to customise God.

These are only some ingredients of a critique of personalised scale. But they illustrate several of the issues that new (and old) Christians will need to address as part of their discipleship. If new entrants to faith are to become counter-cultural, they will need to think through what dimensions of the individually wrapped world they can embrace, what needs to be resisted and how this can be reflected in their everyday lives.

Doing this in a supportive group will give them the strength to journey outward to the world as well as inward to Christ. Just as stressing community will prevent an individualistic faith, so critiquing culture will avoid a pietistic one.

What's wrong with globalisation?

Globalisation promises much – more wealth for example, international cooperation to protect the environment and promote peace, and stronger connections between people all round the world. But Christians might also complain that . . .

- It concentrates power in fewer hands. Giant markets encourage giant companies with giant power. These companies have their own agendas. Will they use their power for the common good?
- It's getting faster and faster. Better communications means that an innovation can be copied quickly 5,000 miles away. Firms have less time to make a profit on their new ideas. So they are under huge pressure to squeeze costs, forcing them to cut corners on the environment and personal relationships.
- It is widening the gap between rich and poor. Larger markets mean larger rewards for the people that win. In almost every occupation, an élite is pulling away from the middle and leaving the bottom behind.

- It is reducing everything to economics. As the market mentality spreads, everything is assigned a price. The value of anything can be measured by its monetary worth. Things which can't be given a price are more easily ignored. But what price might love fetch?
- It is expanding the number of people individuals are in touch with – at work, on-line and friends left behind when the individual moves on. Along with the faster pace of life, this could cut the time spent with close friends. This would undermine the self-worth that comes from belonging, deprive people of the feedback that says 'we value you' and reduce the opportunity to share problems. People would feel more stressed and insecure.
- It is expanding our appetite for MORE – for more experiences, more fulfilment and more novelty. It gets harder to be satisfied. In years ahead, more people than ever before will be seeking happiness – and fewer will find it.

Leader as coach

He used to work in the City of London. Then in his thirties he gave up his job, moved north and settled on a council estate. 'Making converts' he said, 'is easy. People round us are so full of guilt, they face so many difficulties and they struggle in such a variety of ways that persuading them of God's relevance is no difficulty at all. They are crying out for forgiveness, for help in their lives and for the sense of community provided by church. What is really hard is discipleship. Persuading them to change in response to God's love – that is the difficult bit.'

What style of leadership will help tomorrow's people 'change in response to God's love'? Certainly, there will continue to be some people who will appreciate top-down, 'control and command' leadership. Those who are going through detox and rebuilding their lives, for example, will benefit from a directive approach that sets firm boundaries.

Most others will require a different style. A top-down approach will feel manipulative and alien to the 'it's up to you' culture. They will want greater freedom to find their own way.

But they will not want anarchy – it is uncomfortable to be in a group that feels leaderless. Faced by a bewildering array of possibilities, people will continue to value experts and guides even though, as now, they will be suspicious of them. Most people will respond to leaders who take the initiative but also give them space – who provide a coaching style of leadership for example.

Learning that liberates

Coaching is about helping people to learn rather than teaching them. Instead of viewing people as empty vessels into which teaching has to be poured, coaching sees people more as acorns with potential inside them to grow. It does not assume that individuals have all the answers, but through questioning it encourages people to find the answers for themselves.[3]

It is not so dissimilar to Jesus' method of teaching. His parables conveyed truth but invited hearers to discover it for themselves. They had to work out what the parable meant and how it applied. It was a bottom-up approach that left room to explore the parables in different ways (that is why interpretations have been so varied). Instead of being told what to think, hearers were given permission to enquire. Learning became liberating rather than constraining. Eternal truths were combined with space for the individual.

As we rush into the future, a coaching style of leadership will allow people to explore truth at their own pace and to reach their own conclusions. There will still be room for leaders to present truths, but they will do this in a 'coaching' manner by leaving questions hanging in the air, or by offering alternatives for people to reflect on.

Or they may argue a case, but in an open way. 'This is what the Bible says about cohabitation, this is why we think it makes sense, but we realise that you and your friends think differently. So why don't you pray about it, decide whether this is an issue you need to be thinking about now, work out what you think the Bible says and decide how it applies? Whatever you conclude, we'll respect you.' Leaders can be firm on truth but flexible with people.

A standardised gospel that treats everyone the same will be heard less easily than a gospel which makes room for people's very different spiritual journeys. As organisations learn to relate to people in a more personalised way, church that puts individuals into a straitjacket ('All stand for the next song') will feel less welcoming than church which invites people to be themselves ('If you would like to stand for the next song, please feel free'). A laid-back style will suit a laid-back age.

Teams

This style of leadership will help many entering the faith to take on board its radical demands. But it is a style that requires particular gifts. People with those gifts won't necessarily be good administrators too, or team-builders or see the point of working patiently with other church leaders in the area. As we enter a more complex future, teams of leaders, involving people with different gifts, will be essential.[4]

An inside-out church

So how can we draw people into a faith that is genuinely counter-cultural? We need to help them through the sequence of blessing, belonging, believing and behaving – blessing people where they are by forming church round them, enabling people to feel it is 'their' group so that they belong, helping people to grow into Christian belief at their pace, and encouraging belief to transform individuals' behaviour.

Discipleship will start before conversion. It will build radical values into an enquirers' group from the very beginning. It will create radical expectations of community – Christianity is not an individualistic faith but a corporate one. It will help new Christians to criticise the it-must-fit-me world. And it will adopt a leadership style that enables new Christians to own a radical gospel.

All this may help to create a generation of Christians who convert to the church as well as to Christ, who love the world but also critique it, and who believe in truth but don't impose it. Might these be the Christians to turn church inside out to bring the outside in?

Notes

1 William Abraham, *The Logic of Evangelism*, Hodder & Stoughton, 1989.
2 What follows is only the beginnings of a critique of the it-must-fit-me world. I hope to write more on this in due course.
3 See for example John Whitmore, *Coaching for Performance*, Nicholas Brealey, 1992.
4 For a fuller introduction to some of the leadership issues involved in church planting, see Stuart Murray, *Church Planting. Laying Foundations*, Paternoster, 1998, pp. 231–58.

CHAPTER TWELVE

WIZARDS OF THE NEW[1]

In many parts of the advanced world the future of the church is on a knife-edge. All the figures point to the shrivelling up of church – in some places very soon. But we have also seen that there could be a different approach to church which, if blessed by the Spirit, would lay the foundations for growth. Which future takes place depends on the decisions taken by leaders in the local and wider church. Will they become experts at catapulting fresh forms of church?

Smaller churches

Many small church leaders are frantically busy just keeping their heads above water. Often a minister will be responsible for several congregations and will spend life dashing from one service to another, or from one committee to the next. Small congregations may have few people with the gifts and time to support the minister, and so what help is available is devoted to maintaining the status quo. New forms of church, it seems, may never get a look in.

But there is also good news. A survey – yet to be published – of over 8,000 British churches found a clear link between congregational size and the probability of growth. The smaller the congregation in 1989 the more likely it was to have grown over the following decade. Three-fifths of congregations with ten people or less had grown for example against one-fifth of congregations with 51 to 100 members, against only one-tenth of congregations with 400 plus members.[2]

So if you are in a smaller church, take heart! Your prospects are better than for the big boys. What might you do to encourage growth?

Initiatives by lay people?

Some small congregations may be surprised by the untapped potential in their midst. Perhaps there is someone who attends church weekly, but is not involved in other ways. 'Churchy' activities like flower rotas don't appeal. Yet drawing some friends together for a fortnightly coffee morning, to explore spirituality with the minister, might be just her thing.

One hairdresser belonged to a cell church. She complained that she could never invite her friends to the cell because they would not feel comfortable. But when asked about some of the ladies whose hair she looked after, and whether she could invite them to pray with her about family and other issues, she readily agreed, 'especially if I promised to do the praying'. Might that have become the launch-pad for a small group to explore Christianity through prayer, and to evolve into a tiny congregation meeting 'outside church'?

A small church could review its activities. Does it run a luncheon club, perhaps as its main function during the week? Might the group give permission for a short talk at the end of lunch? Could this be a starting-point for the group – if it wished – to explore Christianity, and in due course to evolve into a small worshipping community?

The Y Course – for those not ready for Alpha

- Designed for people 'who don't know the difference between an Epistle and an Apostle'.
- Introduces people to Christian belief.
- Encourages discussion and friendships over eight sessions.
- Quotes from today's culture to support Christian claims.
- Gives plenty of time for people to grasp what's new.
- Covers barriers to belief, like suffering and the claims of other faiths.
- Provides sharply-focused introductions to each session on video, Participants Notes, a Course Leader's Handbook and a Group Leader's Guide (for discussion group leaders) – all in a 'non-cringe' style.
- Could be used as a pre-Alpha course.

Details available from Christian bookshops.

Working with others

Most ministers meet with colleagues nearby from time to time. Frequently these gatherings are helpful in providing mutual support, but they can also feel rather aimless. There is plenty of chat, but little action. Some ministers drop out because it is 'just another meeting', which can discourage those who persevere.

Yet these meetings could spearhead a strategic approach to mission in the area, identifying groups of people that the churches might reach and involving lay people in the process. This would lift from smaller churches the burden of having to resource mission on their own. Sharing resources between churches might create the opportunity for congregational planting beyond the ability of any one church. Cooperation might draw ministers more closely together, countering the isolation that some clergy feel.

But who might have the time and energy to launch a new congregation? Perhaps there is an entrepreneurial minister in the area who feels frustrated by the lack of opportunities in their own church. Such clergy can become deeply discouraged and end up a shadow of their former selves. Sparking new forms of church might release their vision and gifts.

Or a lay person – perhaps a respected head teacher – who has taken early retirement could be the catalyst for a local initiative.

Resources from outside the area

Ministers may be able to draw on resources from outside the area.

When, in collaboration with other churches, we revamped our teenage congregation in Taunton, we asked the Church of England's regional youth officer to provide lots of support. His involvement was immensely helpful and was welcomed by the other churches involved.

About twelve of the Baptist Associations in England, each covering around 50 churches, have a full-time District Missioner. During the 1990s the Missioner in the West Midlands was a catalyst for researching the area, initiating a church plant and gathering a team to lead it.

Why shouldn't local churches working together request support from one or more of their denominations? In the Anglican church, for example, it is customary for newly ordained clergy to work as trainee ministers – curates – for three to four years. It might be possible for local churches to request that a curate in the area be assigned for half of his or her work schedule to a team that was planting a new congregation. This could be an important part of the curate's training.

Church planting teams

Resources could also be available from mission agencies or other organisations. Urban Expression, already referred to, is an initiative of Spurgeon's College and Oasis Trust. It places teams of mainly young people in under-churched areas of East London, to work towards sharing the gospel with people around them. Though still in its infancy, it could be a model for other organisations to build on.

Planting teams that work with local churches could be pivotal in revitalising church. Teams might be responsible for raising their own financial support, or they could be funded by the churches they worked with, or they could receive support through a mission agency, or they could rely on a combination of these. Once a new congregation had been established, some of the original team might form the nucleus of a new one.

So however tough the present, the future need not be bleak for smaller churches. No church need be too small to help spawn a new congregation. Just by being involved with other churches and providing prayer support, any church could play a strategic role.

Larger churches

Larger churches can appear more 'successful' than smaller ones, but scratch beneath the surface and success may be something of an illusion. Where there is growth, it may be due to people transferring from other churches. More often than not, size disguises the fact that large churches have seen little growth, or have even shrunk. The survey quoted earlier found that large congregations were overwhelmingly less likely to have grown in the 1990s than small ones.[3]

Does this mean that big church leaders must give up in despair? Quite the reverse! What they must do is to build into their churches a stronger small church feel. Presumably smaller churches are growing because there is a stronger sense of belonging. Newcomers don't get lost in the crowd and old-timers cannot drift away unnoticed.

In the 1970s and '80s many larger churches introduced home

'Success may be something of an illusion.'

groups to reproduce this element of smallness alongside their big congregations. But in the 1990s the rush of life has made it increasingly difficult to sustain these groups. Many churches have found their home groups withering away. Has the time come for larger churches to establish smaller congregations instead, so that smallness is not an optional extra but built into each person's regular worship? Might there be ways of doing this evangelistically?

Turning activity into mission

Large churches can be a hive of activity, with one initiative following another. But how effective is all this busy-ness in missionary terms? Much of it may have the potential to be extremely effective, but often the potential has yet to be realised.

Perhaps a church runs a coffee shop. The team may pray together at the start of each day. Generosity may be their distinguishing mark – not just generosity of servings, but generosity of time. Waiters or waitresses may continue talking to a customer, knowing that other staff will cover their duties. The coffee shop acquires a reputation for friendliness and attracts a substantial clientele, especially perhaps of lonely people.[4]

But the bridge into church is never built. Non-churchgoers enjoy the coffee shop, but no one makes the leap to Sunday worship. What might the coffee shop do? Using the friendships established during the day, the staff might invite customers to a Bereavement Group, or an Agnostics Anonymous Group or a Better Lifestyle Group in the evening. Rather than being another stepping-stone into mainstream church, the hope would be that the group would evolve into a small congregation in its own right. Would it work? It might be worth a try. Even if the group did not evolve into a congregation, it would still have value in its own right.

Large churches frequently have lots of activities for people on the fringe. Ten years ago a London suburban church started a Wednesday luncheon club for older people. Numbers have grown from a handful to around 80. They introduced a keep-fit class before lunch on alternating weeks, and in the intervening ones started a group for those who wanted to explore the Bible.

Around 30 people now attend that group. Many never go to Sunday church, but on Wednesdays they are studying the Bible and beginning to pray. For them, this is their church. It would not take much to introduce some regular worship, communion from time to time, baptisms (or reaffirmation of baptism vows) and other attributes of a congregation. Teach them to tithe – and they could pay for a part-time pastor for retired people.

Many other churches have groups, not necessarily among older people, that are not in a dissimilar position. Do they have the potential to evolve into a small congregation? This might be a more helpful way of supporting people on their spiritual journeys than struggling to get them to church on Sunday.

Every member missionary

Poynton Baptist Church, a large church in Manchester, England has adopted a different strategy. Members are being encouraged to team up with others who share a similar interest, or who work or live near each other. As a first step, three friends are organising three streams of monthly events – a crafts evening alternating with a film evening; a balanced life-style evening with guided discussions on themes like time out, relationships, managing money and employment; and a laid-back discovery Bible study, in which the golden rule is that each person's views are to be respected.

Someone may come to a pottery evening for example and hear about the other events. As he feels comfortable in the group, he may join them for the next month's film evening, and then for one of the discussions on life-style balance. Eventually through friendships he may be drawn into the discovery Bible study.

There are no plans to attract newcomers into a main church. Rather, as friends invite friends, it is hoped that a congregation will be established with its own way of doing things. The home church's role will be to resource its members (with training and other forms of support) as they become missionaries and church planters. It is still early days, but other groups are in the pipeline, including a group for those who work in the City of Manchester.

This could be a model for other large churches with the staff to catalyse and support such groups. A church might look for ways of freeing up some of its members to form church planting teams in places where they work, among their neighbours or among friends with a similar interest.

In September 2000 All Saints and St Winifrid's Totton, Hampshire, celebrated the first anniversary of their cell church, known as All Saints Everywhere. Groups meet in people's homes during the week and are aimed at non-churchgoers. In the first year numbers attending have swelled from eight to over 50, and two new groups are being formed to accommodate the extra numbers.[5]

Set people free from other church tasks, lift from them the expectation that they invite their friends to mainstream church, immerse them in prayer, support them with advice, training and a shoulder to cry on, and see what happens: new congregations might emerge. In our time-starved world, church planting needn't be another activity on top of work and leisure; it could become an integral part of work and leisure.

Here for you

Smaller churches can be suspicious of larger ones. Sometimes big churches entice people away from smaller ones by offering a higher standard of music or preaching, or a wider range of activities. They may stand aloof from churches in the same locale because they are so tied up with their own programmes. Or other churches may fear that the 'big beasts' will dominate joint ventures.

However, large churches could be an important resource for smaller ones. Thomas Crookes in Sheffield is exploring a 'Minster' model, in which it would provide support for churches nearby. This might include support for ministers, the provision of training and encouraging its own members to serve churches where their gifts were specially needed.

If churches in a town or group of villages had a vision for planting congregations among unreached people, this 'Minster' strategy might be a way for large churches to support them. Offering this support in a control-free way, with few strings attached, would be a demonstration of grace by the more powerful church.

Not only, then, might a larger church plant new congregations among its fringe, or encourage its members to become church planters among their friends: it might help other churches do the same.

Denominational leaders

Who might ignite change within the church? Obviously local leaders have a crucial role, but so too have denominational leaders – bishops, moderators and superintendents for example. Unfortunately some of these more senior people have other priorities, while others believe that their most effective role is to bless new initiatives on the ground – the impetus for change should come from below.

Yet how many problem-schools, hospitals or companies are transformed by senior managers who just bless what's happening below? There is a mass of evidence that proactive leadership is vital. In schools for example standards are not raised by headteachers who simply pat the heads of staff who are doing well. Heads must actively promote best practice and change the culture of the school.[6] When a company is in trouble, a new chief executive is hired to actively turn it round.

Why should church be any different? Faced by further decline and even extinction in some places, it is essential that more leaders provide the impetus for change.

Changing the culture

Leaders of the denominations need to work with their clergy to change their expectations. Over the past ten years in Britain and Australia for example many leaders have been highly successful in putting evangelism on to the local church's agenda. Has the time come to be more radical?

One step might be for a denominational leader to hold a series of meetings with their ministers in a particular area. The aim would be to develop a vision for the locality. Along with items raised by the local ministers, on the agenda would be whether a paradigm shift in ways of being church was needed, and how to cooperate with other denominations.

The denominational leader might explain the rationale for new forms of church, allow time for the others to mull it over, respond to objections, give freedom for the ministers to reshape the concept and work with them to include it as one element in their vision. Just as the best headteachers change the culture of their schools by collaborating with their staff, so the denominational leader would aim to change the culture of church by working jointly with fellow ministers. Once change had begun to take root, the leader might repeat the process in another area.

This will not always be practical, and may be easier for some denominations than for others. But there are encouraging examples of local churches adopting a more strategic approach to their localities. In the Church of England for instance some deaneries, representing the churches in one area, have begun to think more strategically in mission terms. Might some of these be ready to embrace fresh forms of church?

What about a deanery 'Resources and Opportunities Fund', for example, to which local churches could contribute, and which would be used specifically for innovative expressions of church?

Redeploying staff

In some denominations the hierarchy has considerable influence over the appointment of ministers. Where that is so, at the very least a policy might be adopted that only staff who were committed to collaborative mission with other churches would be appointed. Sometimes when ministers are doing this, ways might be found to keep them in the post for longer than might be considered normal. It can take time to establish networks and build trust, and a rapid turnover of staff may undermine local cooperation.

Are there opportunities to redeploy staff so that new forms

of church can be resourced? Hereford diocese in the Church of England has agreed that the bishop should allocate one full-time post to a mission activity. Why not adopt an incremental approach, and every three or four years redeploy one full-time post to launch a new form of church? This could be supplemented by redesigning some other full-time jobs, so that half the person's time was spent on church planting.

Some denominations are ordaining ministers who remain in full-time secular employment. Typically they serve the local church in their spare time. In the Church of England for instance there are a growing number of 'non-stipendiary' and 'ordained local ministers', whose ministry is focused on the local church. Some of these may have the time and expertise to spearhead new congregations, perhaps including congregations at work.

But where church planting requires full-time ministers to spend less time with existing church, non-stipendiary or ordained local ministers may help to fill the gap.

A football fans' church?

Talk about redeploying staff, why not appoint a chaplain to the fans of Manchester United football club for example? The chaplain would be a passionate supporter with considerable knowledge and charisma. His task would be not to entice people into an existing church, but to form a new congregation among United supporters.

Perhaps he would join his mates for a beer, travel with them to every match and become a leading figure in the supporters' club – an ideal job for someone! Then he might meet regularly with a few of his friends, possibly to discuss ways of having a better family life.

As some of his mates are drawn gradually into the faith, they might meet together for prayer, Bible study and worship in a style appropriate to them. The beginnings of a church would form. Other United fans might discover that 'my sort of person' goes to church, and join too.

This would be church growth – where people are.

Too many congregations?

It has been argued[7] that some places have too many congregations already, and that our resources are already over-stretched. Too few ministers are propping up too many near-empty churches. Unless we close down existing congregations, won't planting new forms of church just add to the problem? Resources will be spread so thinly that church will not be viable.

In fact, British churches have been closing at a substantial rate – an average of six a week for the last 20 years.[8] Some would suggest that we accelerate the trend to free up resources for innovative church.

Some of the smallest churches, however, contain worshippers who have been faithful over many years: is it fair to close them down? They also contain some people who are hanging on to faith by their fingernails: is it right to take away their support? Some people who give regularly to church might drift away, reducing the resources available. More small churches are growing than large ones.

Ordained local ministers in the Church of England, who serve the local church in their spare time, will enable many smaller churches to stay open – and some of these may discover new opportunities to grow. Might the church have stumbled, accidentally perhaps, on a way of releasing full-time clergy into new forms of church without having to withdraw pastoral support for an existing church? Certainly any strategy for growth will need to affirm both emerging church and traditional church.

Redeploying staff will be highly problematic and very painful, but any serious strategy for revitalising church will have to face the challenge. What company would employ its best managers in a factory making products that no one wanted to buy? Yet some denominations appoint their best ministers to congregations that no one wants to attend. Is it surprising that in many places the church stares extinction in the face?

Selecting and training leaders

In selecting ministers, many denominations now place greater emphasis on commitment to and aptitude for evangelism. Training reflects this priority too. But if the denominations are to embrace a new paradigm for church, they will need to go further.

The next generation of church leaders will need to include people with the gift of working with others to plant innovative forms of church. They will need to be catalysts, collaborators and coaches – not jealous of those around them, but affirming their gifts and eager to link them with other people.

It is a vital question: are existing arrangements for selecting and training church leaders adequate for this? How much room is there for entrepreneurs? What vision for the future does the wider church have, and are we selecting leaders with the gifts to achieve it and giving them the right training?

Ripe for a makeover

As we look at today's plodding church, we may wonder if it can make the quantum leap into tomorrow. Yet as numbers continue to fall there are signs of a new realism – a recognition that we cannot go on as we are. There is a spiritual openness among many people: frequently it is not God who is the barrier, but church.

Yet maybe church could become attractive again. It will do so not if it sees people as the means to an evangelistic end, but if it values them for their intrinsic worth. The new forms of church being trialled offer some grounds for hope. Can we build on them to develop a new paradigm for church?

Time for change

A new approach is needed if we are to evangelise the advanced world – church that is based not on 'you come to us' but on 'we'll come to you', that is willing to build congregations wherever people are, whether at work or in the shopping mall or in the dance club. We need church that is focused not just on Sundays, but holds its main meetings at any time of the week.

We need church that relies for growth not only on missionary congregations, but on missionaries – and missionary teams. We need local churches who don't do mission on their own, but do it together. We need to take church out to people and plant it where they are – outreach not in-drag, collaborative churches not solo ventures.

Scripture requires it

What drives this strategy is not just that it is likely to work. More important is that it mirrors the New Testament. The earliest church planters did not expect people to come to them. They went to people where they lived, they planted congregations within existing networks, and they promoted unity between those networks by emphasising communication and mutual support.

As today's church gets pushed to the edge of society, its minority position increasingly echoes that of the New Testament church. Is it surprising that its approach to mission should be similar too?

It is theologically imperative that we do church differently to the way we do it now. When God in Jesus came to the world, he immersed himself in the culture where he lived. When the first Christians planted churches, they immersed those churches in the cultures where their converts lived. Over the next 2,000 years many other Christians have done the same.

It is time for the advanced world church to recapture this vision and make church culturally current once again. Only then will church have the strength to transform society.

Fresh church for a new world

That sounds a far cry from much of church today. But some changes are afoot. Would it take much for this trickle to become a flood? It only needs small steps, adapting what's been tried and building on what exists, for local and national leaders to become catalysts for change.

If we remain as we are we face near extinction in the years ahead. It is time for a church makeover, time to become a fresh church for an it-must-fit-me world.

Notes

1 On-line Multi-User Domains often rely on experts, 'wizards', to help newcomers and facilitate the group.
2 Peter Brierley, 'Church Growth in the 1990s. Statistical Report'. I am grateful to the Rev'd Bob Jackson, who has collaborated with this research, for making these provisional figures available to me.
3 Of course, size of congregation need not equate to size of church. A large church might have lots of small congregations – a strategy that makes eminent sense in the light of these figures.
4 A number of larger churches run coffee shops, as do most cathedrals in Britain. This description is based on the practice of a Christian coffee shop in an Oxfordshire village.
5 *The Winchester Way*, October 2000.
6 Some of this evidence is summarised by Michael Barber, *The Learning Game*, Victor Gollancz, pp. 129*ff.*
7 e.g. by Robin Gill in respect to Britain. For a summary see Robin Gill, *A Vision for Growth*, SPCK, 1994, pp. 62–79.
8 Brierley, *op. cit.*, p. 195.